THE LIGHT FORCE

OUTRAGEOUS OBJECT LESSONS

E.G. Von Trutzschler

Illustrated
by
Tom Finley

Published by Gospel Light Publications, Ventura, California 93006. Printed in U.S.A.

THE ART
OF DEMONSTRATING
THE LESSON

I trust this book will be more than a typical book of object lessons. It was written to bring a new and creative approach to two common problems teachers have with their students: lagging interest and missing the point. I've included a variety of stories, illustrations, and analogies that I have used and found successful in generating both interest and understanding. If used properly and creatively, these object lessons can bring a new vitality and clarity to your teaching, too.

Von

Rights for publishing this book in other languages are contracted by Gospel Literature International (GLINT) foundation. GLINT also provides technical help for the adaptation, translation, and publishing of Bible study resources and books in scores of languages worldwide. For further information, contact GLINT, Post Office Box 488, Rosemead, California 91770, U.S.A., or the publisher.

Dear Reader:

The object lessons in this book may spark your creative abilities in many ways. You may use some of the objects suggested to illustrate more than one truth (examples of this can be found in the sections using traps, vines, or branches). You may find new twists to the illustrations to clarify pertinent Bible truths for your group. And, because every leader's style, students, and situation is unique, you may find that a slight change in the staging of one of the object lessons makes it more effective for you. Use the material given in this book in a way that will enhance your particular needs, teaching style, and originality.

Like all LIGHT FORCE products, **Outrageous Object Lessons** is designed to be an effective ministry tool that can be used simply, just as it was written, or as a launch pad for your own creativity.

THE OBJECT LESSON

Object lessons have gotten a bum rap! For years, they've been stuffed in the closet of the children's primary department along with crayons, scissors, and flannelgraph boards. Many people who teach youths and adults think that object lessons are beneath them. Little kids' stuff. That's too bad. Actually, object lessons are best suited for use with youths and adults because they have a greater capacity than children to comprehend the abstract scriptural truths that object lessons illustrate, clarify, and reinforce. And here's more good news: object lessons also command attention, build interest, and add variety to a lesson. Those are all welcome benefits for the average teacher struggling to communicate to students who are used to the fast-paced visual imagery of TV.

Here's another interesting point about object lessons: they aren't "Johnny come latelies" on the teaching scene. God made the prophet Jeremiah a walking, talking object lesson. (If you ever run short of object lesson ideas, just take a look through the book of Jeremiah!) And Jesus employed object lessons to reinforce the truths He taught. He used a grapevine to illustrate the important concept of abiding in Him. He used a farmer sowing seed to illuminate the concept of the gospel's work and growth in the believer's heart. Jesus knew that if a person could visualize a concept, he or she would be more likely to understand it. He also knew the value of keeping the attention of the people He taught.

Teachers today can learn some important lessons from Jeremiah and Jesus. Like them, teachers are trying to communicate biblical concepts—and that's not an easy task. Teachers appreciate and want to keep their students' attention because a person who is interested is more likely to learn. But almost every teacher has experienced that sinking feeling in the pit of the stomach when he or she looks into the faces of the class members and sees attention and interest slipping away. A review of Jesus' teaching techniques and a plan to put some of them into practice during the next class will help remedy the situation.

Spiritual food, like physical food, needs to be balanced with variety. Jesus avoided the boredom of predictability by using stories, illustrations, analogies, examples, and object lessons, to help keep the attention of the people He taught and to help them better understand spiritual truths.

To keep your classroom from becoming a predictably boring place where you teach a predictably boring lesson, add variety. Look for ways to reinforce and enliven your teaching with stories, illustrations, examples, analogies, and yes, object lessons.

The potential for creating and developing object lessons is almost unlimited. They are available and often inexpensive. This manual provides 46 object lessons that have been used successfully. Try them out and see how they add interest and put a little kick back into your teaching.

CONTENTS

USING THE OBJECT LESSON

Object lessons are in a class of learning all their own. Distinct and different, they add a refreshing dimension to teaching. An object lesson can move your students from interest, to understanding, and then on to application.

Using object lessons requires the unique skill of making the most of simple analogies. As you prepare to teach an object lesson, you will need to look at an object, think about it, and discover ways the object applies to the lesson you're teaching. Then you will need to determine the best time to use the object lesson as you teach. Your students will not only hear the words you say, they *see* a concept and therefore understand it better.

Here are some suggestions to help you start using object lessons as you communicate God's truth.

BE CONFIDENT: Students pick up quickly on a teacher who is unsure and nervous. You can be confident that a demonstration of a point in your lesson (an object lesson) will be well received by your students.

BE PREPARED: "Be prepared" isn't just a Boy Scout motto, it also should be the motto of every teacher. Plan your lesson and the object lesson carefully. Remember, you must understand the principle of the object lesson before you can effectively share it with others. To be adequately prepared, you will have to run through your object lesson a couple of times before you present it to the class. Then, as you leave home, *check* to be sure you have everything you need. Nothing will set you back like an object lesson for which you don't have all the objects!

ANTICIPATE REACTION: Often an object lesson will produce an immediate and obvious reaction from your students. You are looking for a reaction that indicates that they have caught the concept. If you know your demonstration and your group, anticipating reactions is fairly easy. Jumps, screams, or other reactions you haven't anticipated, can throw you off balance and interrupt the flow of the lesson or the impact of the application. Anticipating such reactions pays. It will help you keep cool and work the reactions to your advantage.

DON'T OVERUSE THEM: Often when people discover a good thing, they overuse it. You can overuse object lessons. They seem to work so well that you may want to share one every time you teach. Use your judgment. You will keep the value of object lessons high if you don't overuse them. Don't allow object lessons to become an easy way to entertain your group.

USE THEM AS PART OF THE LESSON: An object lesson boosts interest and clarifies a lesson point. The object lesson is not the entire lesson.

EMPLOY SURPRISE: Surprise is a valuable asset in any lesson. In most cases it pays to keep your "object" out of sight. You may have to get to your class or meeting early in order to conceal the object before students arrive. However, there are times when leaving an unusual object in sight stimulates curiosity. Interest is what you are after. You will want to stimulate it in the way that seems best: by surprise, by curiosity, or by shock!

USE COMMON SENSE: Common sense (which isn't too common today), is an invaluable asset as you develop an effective object lesson and personalize it to your group's needs. Think about what you want to demonstrate and clarify. Take the ideas in this manual, use them and expand on them— but be sure to use a liberal amount of common sense!

BORROW: As you search for the right objects to use in your demonstrations, you may be able to borrow some items. (Borrowing keeps down the cost.) It pays to search around. Most of the items aren't hard to find. When you have borrowed an object, use it carefully and return it *promptly* with a thank you.

CONSIDER THE COST: Some object lessons may be expensive to present. But you get what you pay for in life. If you want IMPACT!—a lasting lesson—be willing to pay for it. However, consider this: many object lessons make a greater and more lasting impact than a film, yet they almost always cost less. When it comes to a life-changing concept or lesson, don't pinch pennies.

In the following pages, you will find many new and fresh object lesson ideas. Use them and see how they will perk up your class and make your communication of God's truth more effective.

THE COLD HEART

PRINCIPLE:

Our hearts can grow cold toward God.

FOOD FOR THOUGHT:

Psalms 44:20,21; 101:5; Proverbs 16:5; 28:14; Jeremiah 17:10; Matthew 13:15; 24:12; Romans 1:21; 2:5; Hebrews 3:8,12

LESSON:

The heart is an interesting subject. Today, hearts show up in many different places. We see them taking the place of the word "love" on bumper stickers. Hearts seem to be everywhere on Valentine's Day. We hear about mechanical hearts. And, of course, each of us has a heart. Without any direct thought or effort on our part, it keeps right on pumping. A beating heart is essential to life itself.

In His Word, God speaks about the heart. He refers to it as the center of the person. God says the heart controls the way a person thinks and acts. The Bible describes people whose hearts are right in relation to God. It also talks about people whose hearts are cold and indifferent toward God and His interests. A Christian's cold-hearted indifference to God can show up in many ways. Sometimes the person loses interest and enthusiasm for God and church, and for his or her Christian brothers and sisters. Studying God's Word may become a boring, tedious task to a person with a cold heart. Eventually, the person begins searching for things other than God, His Word, and His desires for him or her. A cold heart feels out of place and looks ugly.

What can we do about a cold heart? First, we must recognize that the condition exists. And that we've lost our first love for God. The next step isn't hard—it's coming back to a loving, forgiving God; it's taking another look at who He is and who we are, and realizing that we can only be happy when we have a heart that is warm for Him and His purpose for us.

A cold, unbeating heart is a sign that a Christian is out of touch with God—his or her source of life, warmth and joy. However, a heart that loves God and wants to do His will brings excitement and enthusiasm to the individual, as well as to the group.

To keep a physical heart pumping and healthy, it's a good idea to exercise and to eat the right kinds of food. To keep a spiritual heart alive and warm toward God, it must be guarded from the diseases sin and indifference bring to it. And most of all, it must be fed and exercised regularly with God's Word, prayer, and care and concern for others.

MATERIALS NEEDED:

One heart (preferably the heart of a lamb or goat; a cow's heart will be too large), paper towels, plastic wrap, a paper bag.

INSTRUCTIONS:

At home, wash the heart in cool water then pat it dry with paper towels. Wrap it in plastic wrap. Refrigerate the wrapped heart until you are ready to take it to class. Before you leave home, place the heart in a paper bag to conceal it until it's time to use it. As you begin speaking about the cold heart, remove the heart from the sack and allow the group to pass it around so that each person may hold it and examine it closely. When everyone has seen the heart, take it back and hold it as you continue to speak. Be prepared for some screams and comments about how gross the heart is. Plan for ways to control the group's enthusiasm. Be sure to take the heart with you when you leave.

TRUST ME!

PRINCIPLE:

We are to trust God and His Word.

FOOD FOR THOUGHT:

Psalm 62:8; 112:7; 118:8; Proverbs 3:5; 16:20; Mark 4:40; John 20:29; Ephesians 3:12; 2 Timothy 1:12; Hebrews 10:23

LESSON:

We live in a world full of deception—a world in which it is hard to trust or to believe anyone. People make promises and don't keep them. When we take people at their word and trust them, only to find that we've been deceived once again, we may feel like we have been made to look foolish. We may become suspicious of others and their motives. Often people develop an attitude of "I'll believe it when I see it!"

Our distrust carries over into our attitudes toward God. We don't see Him, so we have a hard time believing Him. He tells us in His Word that He loves us and has our best interests in mind. But it's not always easy to believe Him.

As we get to know God better, we find that we trust Him more and more as we discover that He always keeps His promises. He really does have our best interests in mind.

MATERIALS NEEDED:

A rattrap, light-gauge wire or a soldering iron and solder, a ten-dollar bill which you are prepared to give away.

INSTRUCTIONS:

Set your trap, holding it securely with one hand. Then wire or solder the spring lever to the bait tongue so that the trap won't spring. Be careful as you work because the trap must look as if it is set to go off. Test the trap to make sure it is safe. Then place the ten-dollar bill on the bait tongue.

At the beginning of the object lesson, casually show the group the "baited" trap. Ask who would like to take the money. As you offer it to the students, you will find that they're frustrated—as much as they want the money, they won't take the "bait." Explain that they won't get hurt. As you speak to the group, ask one person if he trusts you. If the answer is yes, ask the person to take you at your word. The money will be his only if the person will take it off the trap. When someone finally trusts you and takes the money, the other group members' reaction will be well worth your effort and money. Your students will understand that you knew all along that no harm would come to them, and that the money was a special gift for anyone who would believe your promise and respond in trust.

After the demonstration, make your application as suggested in the lesson.

FEELINGS, FEELINGS!

PRINCIPLE:

We cannot base our faith on feelings.

FOOD FOR THOUGHT:

Psalm 112:7; Proverbs 3:5,21-26; Matthew 7:24-27; Romans 10:17; James 1:6,7; 1 John 2:17

LESSON:

In World War II, thousands of airplanes were in use, many of them bombers. The pilots and aircraft were pushed to the extreme limits of endurance, going almost day and night. Of course, many planes crashed. As these crashes were investigated, a mystery began to develop. Many of the

12

planes weren't hit by gunfire. They hadn't run out of fuel. They'd just crashed. As the experts studied the situation, they solved the mystery. Vertigo—a state in which a person is dizzily disoriented—was the culprit.

When over-tired pilots became confused and disoriented, they didn't believe or trust their instruments. They began to fly their planes by feeling. And ultimately, they would crash and burn.

A pilot flying in the dark or dense fog has only his instruments to rely on. His altimeter, airspeed, horizon compass, and fuel indicators tell him what's going on. Often, a tired pilot will have an overwhelming feeling that he is really going one direction when the compass indicates another, or that he is really at a much higher altitude than the altimeter shows. If he begins flying according to his feeling rather than the instruments, he is due for a crash.

Feelings are important. But today, we often hear the message, "If you don't feel it, it isn't real!" That's a dangerous statement! Many Christians crash their lives because of spiritual vertigo. They are flying through life on feelings. But feelings are fickle. They can be affected by lack of sleep, foods, moods, circumstances—any number of things. The Word of God is the Christian's "instrument panel." We can trust the instruments God has given us, even if it doesn't "feel right."

Most of us crash when things cloud up in our lives, storms develop, and we experience the ups and downs of turbulence. We lose our orientation and are forced to trust God's Word, God's instruments. That's when we are tempted to doubt God. We are tempted to make decisions based on our feelings alone. Yet, that is when it is more important to trust the Word. Trust the instruments. Fly the straight course of faith until we pull out of the storm. And pull out we will. If we become panicky and try to correct our lives according to our feeling alone, the ultimate end will be to crash and burn! We must keep our feelings in proper perspective and learn to trust God and His Word. It's the only way to fly!

MATERIALS NEEDED:

A large model or toy airplane; if possible, a horizon compass or altimeter.

INSTRUCTIONS:

Hold the airplane so everyone can see it. Refer to it from time to time as you make your points about flying. If you have a compass and altimeter, display and refer to them at appropriate times.

DYNAMIC REACTION

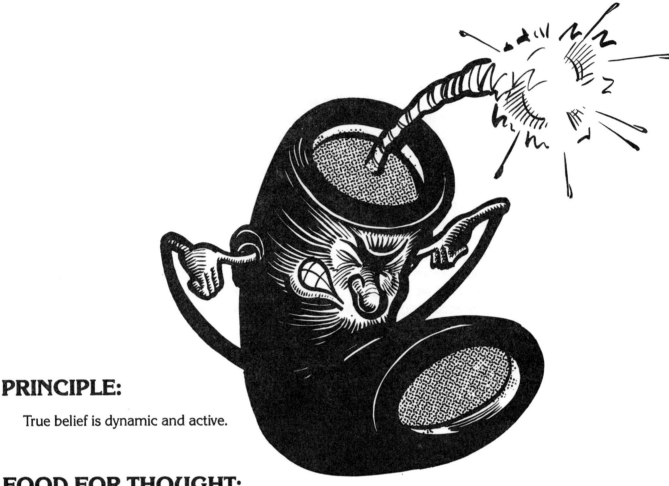

PRINCIPLE:

True belief is dynamic and active.

FOOD FOR THOUGHT:

Matthew 8:8-13; 17:20; Mark 5:28-34; Acts 15:26; Ephesians 1:17-19; 3:16-20;
1 Thessalonians 1:3-9

LESSON:

Today, we Christians call ourselves believers, just as the first followers of Jesus called themselves believers. However, we seem to be lacking some of the dynamic power those first believers had. The disciples were willing to die for their Lord and Saviour, Jesus Christ. And many of them did die for Him! The pages of the New Testament resound with the enthusiasm, zeal, and commitment to Christ of those first believers.

What's the difference between those dynamic believers and today's believers? Perhaps it is that today we have a more academic belief in Jesus, whereas early believers had dynamic, active belief. There's an important difference between academic belief and dynamic, active belief. A person may have an academic belief in that chair. The person believes that the chair exists, that it is made of metal (or wood) and that when he sits on it, it won't collapse. However, that person's belief is actively demonstrated when he actually sits in the chair.

Belief in a chair—even dynamic, active belief—is not going to dramatically change our lives. But moving from academic belief about Jesus Christ to a dynamic, active belief in Him and His power in our lives can move us to a radically different life-style.

MATERIALS NEEDED:

Two medium or large firecrackers, a toothpick, matches.

INSTRUCTIONS:

Careful preparation for this object lesson is crucial! Carefully pull the fuse out of one of the firecrackers. Using a toothpick, work all the powder out of the firecracker. Then turn it upside down and flick it with your finger to remove any powder that might be stuck inside. Take the powder outside and blow it around so it can't be ignited. Then, push the fuse about ½ inch into the empty firecracker. Light the fuse. The firecracker should not go off—but stand back just in case it does. Now that you've tested the firecracker and are sure it won't go off, carefully take the fuse out of the other firecracker. Insert the fuse about ½ inch into the dummy firecracker so that it looks like a live firecracker.

Before the session, place the firecracker and book of matches in your pocket or purse. Then, after you have spoken about dynamic, reactive belief, use the firecracker to demonstrate what you mean. Use explanations similar to the following. "Let me use this firecracker to demonstrate what I mean. Watch carefully as I light the fuse." (Light the fuse. Hold the firecracker for a second or two; then throw it into the group. After a few moments, pick up the firecracker in order to control the excitement your demonstration will generate.) "You had a dynamic reaction when I threw the firecracker at you because you thought the firecracker would go off. You responded according to what you believed. You moved! You showed dynamic, active belief. You did something because of what you believed. You didn't just sit there thinking about it—you acted! That's the kind of belief New Testament Christians had. It's a converting, active belief that will make a difference in our lives. The question is, how many of us really have that kind of belief in Jesus Christ?"

SEEDY CONSEQUENCES

PRINCIPLE:

What you sow, you reap.

FOOD FOR THOUGHT:

Proverbs 22:8; Hosea 8:7; 10:12; 2 Corinthians 9:6; Galatians 6:7,8

LESSON:

In His Word, God says very clearly that we are not to be deceived—whatever we sow, that and that alone shall we reap (see Galatians 6:7,8). That seems understandable. If a person wants to grow watermelons, he's not going to plant just any kind of seeds—he's going to plant watermelon seeds. If he wants to grow radishes, he's not going to plant carrot seeds and figure that radishes will grow. Any farmer—and almost anyone else—knows the principles of sowing and reaping and abides by it.

Sowing and reaping seems to be a fairly simple principle to understand when we're talking about seeds. However, when it comes to sin in our lives, we sometimes forget that the same principle applies: we reap what we sow. Sins are a lot like seeds: when we plant seeds of sin, we can be sure that they will sprout and grow.

There are other ways in which sins are like seeds: sins often come in flashy packages, sins are common and readily available, and most sins seem quite small. They are easy to drop along the way and forget. But in a matter of time, the seeds of sin come up—and the harvest they bring is sadness, heartbreak, and destruction.

Seeds and sins are alike in still another way. Some seeds, like beans and radishes, sprout and grow rapidly. Some sins also sprout and grow rapidly. But there are other seeds, like carrots and lettuce, that take longer to come up. Even though we may forget them, the seeds are still growing; they will come up. Sometimes, because we don't pay the consequences for our sins immediately, we think they've gone away. But, like the slow growing seeds, they are sprouting and developing. They will come up, too.

Here's another interesting fact about seeds: by planting one seed, you'll get more in return. One seed produces a bountiful harvest. For example, if you plant an orange seed, it can grow into a tree that will ultimately produce thousands of oranges. The same is true with apple seeds, radish seeds, corn seeds, bean seeds, etc. Like seeds, sins produce more sins.

We can be sure God knew what He was talking about when He said that a person will reap what he or she sows.

16

MATERIALS NEEDED:

Three or more packages of seeds. (Try to get a variety of large, medium, and small seeds, such as radish, lettuce, corn and bean seeds.)

INSTRUCTIONS:

Place the seed packages in your pocket or purse before class. As soon as you begin comparing seeds and sins, take the packages out one by one. Open each package and pour the seeds into your hand so the students can see them. If possible, cast some of the seeds on the floor as you talk about sowing.

SOME SEED LESSONS

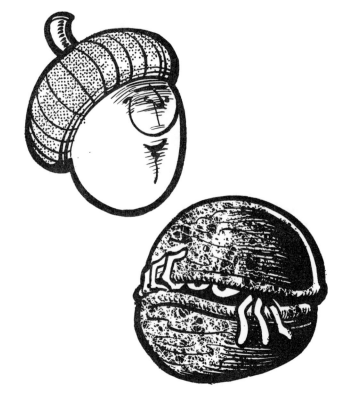

PRINCIPLE:

God has made each person unique, placing in him or her the potential for growth.

FOOD FOR THOUGHT:

Psalm 126:5,6; Hosea 10:12; Matthew 13:3-8; Luke 8:5-15; John 15:8; 1 Corinthians 3:6,7; 2 Corinthians 9:6; Galatians 6:7,8

LESSON:

Many people don't believe in miracles. After all, we don't see many of them. Or do we? "Miracle" is an appropriate term for the handiwork of God we see in nature: The miracle of life, for example. As much as we study and analyze, we can't create life. Life is a mystery. And life shows up in some of the most peculiar places. A seed is a good example. Life is tucked away inside it. When the proper conditions are met, a miracle will happen. The seed will sprout and grow. But if the seed doesn't receive what it needs to grow, eventually it will be unable to do so. The seed will become just an empty shell.

Just as we can't tell what's on the inside of a seed by looking at the shell, we can't tell what a person is really like just by looking at the outside. Yet, many of us are so used to looking at the outward appearances of people that we fail to recognize what's on the inside. We certainly can't tell the potential tucked away inside a person by what he or she looks like. Just like this little seed. It's quite common, rather humble. But it has great potential. Given the right conditions, it can grow into a great tree. Each of us has been given life and we have even greater potential than a seed. We just have to cultivate the right conditions for ourselves so we can flourish and grow. And believe it or not, those conditions really are the things we can control: choosing to love God and study His word, disciplining our thoughts, being careful about the things we read and see, choosing our friends carefully.

18

People are a lot like seeds, really. We are miracles, but too often, we don't realize it. Some of us have very low opinions of ourselves. We seem to think that we'll never amount to anything. But God sees us so differently. He can make any person into a great person, if he or she is just willing to cultivate the right conditions. In order to grow, a seed has to be buried, and actually die, to produce the miracle of a living, growing tree. At first, the little sapling is fragile, but it grows larger and larger until it becomes firm, strong, and very visible. When we are willing to give up our own selfish desires, God is able to produce the miracle of spiritual growth within our lives. God can produce in us growth that is firm, strong, and pleasing to Him. The small can become mighty.

If we look closely at seeds, we discover that they're not the same—each of them is unique. God created each person to be unique, too. Each of us is different because that's how God planned for us to be. It's quite a miracle that God cares about each person so much that He makes each individual unique. After all, wouldn't it be easier to "make a mold" and keep using it?

Seeds help show us the small, seemingly insignificant miracles God is continually working. If we are willing to meet the conditions, God will produce miracles in our lives, too.

MATERIALS NEEDED:

Large nuts, such as acorns, walnuts, or almonds.

INSTRUCTIONS:

Conceal nuts in your pocket or purse. As you speak, take out the nuts one at a time. Hold the nuts in your hands, showing them to the group as you make your points.

WHERE AM I GOING?

PRINCIPLE:

It pays to know where you are going.

FOOD FOR THOUGHT:

Job 23:10-12; Psalm 1:1,2; 32:8; 119:9-11,133; Proverbs 3:6; 16:20

LESSON:

Most of us know what a map is. Not all of us have studied maps, not all of us have used maps, but we all know what a map is. When we walk or drive in familiar areas, we don't need maps. However, when we travel to unfamiliar areas, we need guidance.

Most cars have what we call a "map compartment" or "glove compartment" where maps are kept. But even so, most of us have been with someone who has gotten lost. Or, we've gotten lost ourselves.

Perhaps you or someone you know has had an experience such as this: You're taking a trip to a vaguely familiar place. In anticipation you get the car ready, carefully pack everything that you'll be needing, and plan exactly what you'll do once you get there. Then, you happily set off for your destination without checking a map. After all, you know the general direction and it would take too much time to look at a map. It's much easier just to jump in the car and head out.

But when you come to a strange city you may become disoriented—and lost. Instead of getting out the map and looking at it, you may pull into a service station and ask the attendant for directions. Or you might stop a stranger on the street and ask how to get where you want to go—and the best way to get there.

Many of us live like that. We have a map for our journey through life—God's Word. It gives us all the information we need to successfully travel through life. Yet, we're so anxious and excited about getting on our way that we fail to study God's Word, which could help us take the best route from where we are to where we want to be. Often when we get confused, when we don't quite understand where we should be going, we're more apt to ask people for counsel and advice about where we're going than we are to study God's map—the Bible.

It seems so hard to open the Bible and to study it to get our bearings. Yet, for Christians, that is the most logical thing to do. We really need to learn this lesson. Trying to travel through life without consulting God's map is just like trying to take a long trip without first studying the map and deciding the best way to go. We can't take the trip without getting lost if we don't study the map. We need to take the time to figure out what God's will is by prayerfully studying His Word. It does no more good to carry a closed Bible with us than it does to travel without consulting the map that's folded up in the glove compartment. The Word of God is *the* map for a Christian. We must study it carefully.

MATERIALS NEEDED:

A city or state map.

INSTRUCTIONS:

Before the session, place the map in your pocket or purse. When everyone is seated, pull out the map and open it. Introduce the object lesson by asking questions such as, "Who uses maps?" "Why would a person use a map?" "What might happen if a person used an inaccurate map?" After you have generated interest by discussing the questions, continue with the object lesson. You may illustrate some points in the object lesson by telling about times when you have been lost because you didn't use a map.

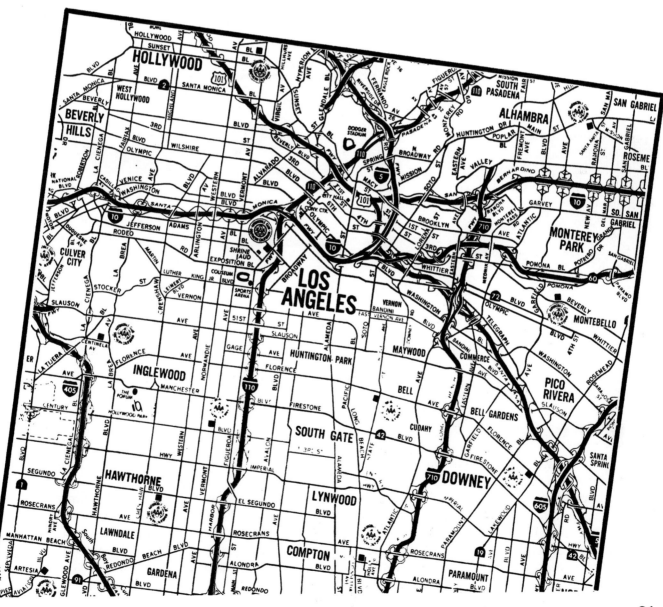

TRAPS SATAN USES

PRINCIPLE:

Satan knows our weaknesses and he will try to enslave us.

FOOD FOR THOUGHT:

Matthew 16:23; 2 Corinthians 2:11; Ephesians 4:27; 5:6-11; 6:11-17; James 1:13-15; 4:7; 1 Peter 5:8; 1 John 3:7-10

LESSON:

People react to traps in different ways: some of us are afraid of them; others are fascinated by them.

There are many different kinds of traps: gopher traps, mousetraps, rattraps, and even cockroach traps. Each kind of trap is designed to catch a particular little (or big) critter. Some traps will destroy their victims; others will only capture them. The person who designed the common mousetrap knew that mice like certain kinds of bait. So, the trap has a tongue on which the bait is placed. When the mouse, not knowing that a trap has been set for it, takes the bait, it gets caught.

Most of us, as Christians, know that we have an enemy named Satan. He uses all sorts of devices and strategies to try to pull us away from fellowship with God, to capture us, and, if possible, to destroy us. One of the devices Satan uses quite successfully is a trap. Satan knows the kind of "bait" we like. He knows what we love, what we are like, the areas in which we are weak. He will bait his traps with those very things. We need to carefully watch for the traps Satan sets for us.

A snare—a rope placed across a path or trail—is another kind of trap. If we're not aware of where we're walking, if we stray from the path the Lord wants us to walk on, Satan can trip us in a snare and put us out of commission fast! And, there's the pit. If we stray from the path, we're apt to fall into the pit.

Satan really wants to hinder us, to enslave us, and to keep us from fellowship with God. He will use any trap he possibly can to do it. We must be careful to be sure we don't become victims by seeing only the bait in the trap and not the conditions that surround it, or by following Christ in a haphazard, lackadaisical way, making ourselves prime candidates for Satan's pits and snares.

MATERIALS NEEDED:

A variety of traps, such as: mousetrap, rattrap, cockroach trap, gopher trap (and, if possible, traps used to catch larger animals such as coyotes); rope or twine to represent the snare; a shovel to represent the pit.

INSTRUCTIONS:

Before the session, conceal all your materials. As you begin your lesson, display the traps. Then at appropriate times as you talk, pick up the traps and demonstrate how they function.

THE RIGHT FREQUENCY

PRINCIPLE:

God uses His Word to speak to us.

FOOD FOR THOUGHT:

Proverbs 18:15; Matthew 13:11-16; John 10:3-5,16; Romans 10:17; 2 Timothy 4:3,4

LESSON:

We all have ears. For some of us, our ears do a very good job. They make it possible for us to hear many different sounds. But for others, ears don't function as well as they should. They may have hearing impairments. There may be sounds they don't hear.

There are some sounds none of us can hear, no matter how good our ears are. For example, people can't hear the noise made by a dog whistle because our ears aren't attuned to such high frequencies.

There are many other frequencies that can't be heard by the unaided ear. Some are beamed in from satellites and broadcast from radio and television stations. Those frequencies carry all kinds of communications: news, music, entertainment shows, educational shows—to name a few. But without the right kind of receiver, tuned to a particular frequency, we can't hear any of them.

A radio is a receiver. When we tune it to a certain frequency, we receive what is being broadcast on that frequency, whether it be news or music or a talk show.

The Bible is similar to a radio receiver, except that the Bible has only one frequency—the frequency that God uses to talk to us. We need the Bible to tune into the messages God has for us. And like a transistor radio, God's Word is portable; we can take it anywhere. We can turn it on anytime by reading it. The Bible gives us stories, information, enjoyment, and blessings. What variety we receive when we tune into God's frequency!

24

MATERIALS NEEDED:

One functional, battery operated transistor radio.

INSTRUCTIONS:

Conceal the radio before the session. As you talk about frequencies, pause, pull out the radio, turn it on loud enough so everyone may hear it, and tune in several stations to demonstrate how the radio receives the different frequencies broadcast by radio stations. Emphasize that none of the sounds could be heard without the proper receiver. When you've made your point, turn off the radio and put it away. Continue the object lesson by making the comparison between a radio and the Bible.

OH, FOR A KEY

PRINCIPLE:

The Holy Spirit teaches us by helping us understand God's Word.

FOOD FOR THOUGHT:

John 14:26; John 16:12-15; 1 Corinthians 2:10-14

LESSON:

We know that the Bible is God's letter to us. It is essential for us, as Christians, to read God's Word because in it God teaches us about Himself and gives us instructions about how we are to live. But all too often the Bible seems to be dry, uninteresting, and just plain boring.

It's easy to watch TV or read an interesting magazine because we enjoy it. Why is the Bible so difficult for many of us to read? Why is it hard for us to understand? Some people enjoy reading the Bible—they even get something from it. What makes the difference? What is the key that unlocks the Bible?

To understand the Bible, we must be Christians. We must believe that the Scriptures are true. We must be willing to read and study them. But the Holy Spirit is the real key to understanding and enjoying the Bible. He is our teacher. He helps us understand what God's Word means. That is why before we study the Bible, we pray, asking God, through the Holy Spirit, to help us understand His Word. Remember, the Holy Spirit is the key that opens our understanding of the Scripture.

MATERIALS NEEDED:

A large lock, one key that fits the lock, five or six additional keys similar in appearance to the first but that don't fit the lock, six or seven round key tags, a stick-on label, a felt pen, a paper sack, a stopwatch or wristwatch with a second hand, pencil and paper, table or desk.

INSTRUCTIONS:

Secure a key tag to each key. On both sides of the key tag attached to the key that fits the lock, print "Holy Spirit." On both sides of the other key tags, print words such as "faith," "education," "knowledge," "discipline," "quiet time," and "anticipation." (Print the same word on both sides of each key tab.) Print "The Bible" on the stick-on label and attach it to the lock. Place the keys and the lock in a paper sack.

Make arrangements for another adult to keep time during the contest described below. Provide him or her with a stopwatch or a wristwatch with a second hand, pencil and paper for keeping score.

Make sure to have a table or desk, cleared off, in another room or in another area of the room in which you will be meeting.

When the group has been seated, ask a group member to place the keys and the lock on the table or desk. Explain to the group that in a few minutes, there will be a contest. Then explain the contest rules: one by one, the students will go to the table and try to discover which key opens the lock. They will be timed; the person who finds the key in the shortest amount of time will be the winner. (If you have a large group, choose volunteers or teams for the contest.)

Begin the object lesson by talking about God's Word. After you have asked the question "What is the key that unlocks the Bible?" begin the contest. When the contest is over, conclude the object lesson by explaining that the Holy Spirit is the key that opens our understanding of the Word.

A LITTLE MIRACLE

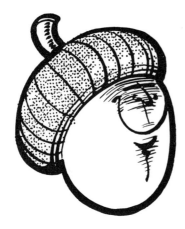 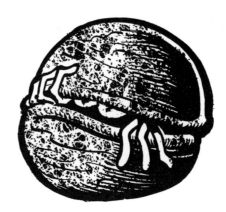

PRINCIPLE:

You can't tell what's on the inside by looking at the outside.

FOOD FOR THOUGHT:

1 Samuel 16:7; Matthew 23:25-28; 2 Corinthians 4:7,16,18

LESSON:

Most of us are impressed by how someone looks on the outside. As a matter of fact, most of us spend a great deal of time working on our "outsides." We're careful about our clothing and our grooming. We're careful about the appearance we make—what kinds of cars we drive, what our houses look like. We take such good care of the outside because that's what people see.

God has a different perspective. He looks at the inside. He's interested in a person's inner qualities. It's too bad we don't look at people in the same way. Usually we're impressed by people who are good-looking. We don't tend to be impressed by people who are ugly, pudgy, or disfigured because we have a tendency to label people by how they look.

Take, for example, a gifted young man with a great personality who was also very attractive. One day, the young man was in a fiery accident. The fire burned his face terribly. When his burns healed, they left disfiguring, ugly scars. His friends no longer wanted to be around him. They didn't like to look at him, so they avoided him. Yet, the man was really the same person. He was still gifted. He still had a great personality. The only thing that had changed was the outside—the way he looked.

We can't really tell what something is like on the inside by looking at the outside. A nut illustrates that fact. The nut is quite common—we probably wouldn't look at it twice. Yet, what potential this seed has tucked away inside it. It contains a miracle. God made this seed so that, under the right conditions, it will grow into a large tree. A strong tree. A very impressive tree.

Many of us are like this seed. We're quite common. We're not that impressive to look at. But we have a miracle within us. God has created us for a purpose; under the right conditions, we will grow into impressive persons who will make an impact on our world.

MATERIALS NEEDED:

A nut, such as an acorn, walnut, or almond.

INSTRUCTIONS:

Place the nut in your purse or pocket. When you begin talking about the nut, take it out and show it to the group.

USED BY GOD

PRINCIPLES:

God made each of us unique because He intends to use each of us differently.

FOOD FOR THOUGHT:

Isaiah 29:16; Isaiah 45:9; Isaiah 64:8; Romans 9:20,21; 2 Corinthians 4:7; Ephesians 2:10

LESSON:

God wants to use us, and we are to serve Him. God speaks of us as vessels, all created to be used in different ways.

Many different kinds of vessels are found in the average kitchen. There are cups and glasses, pots and pans, trash cans and vases. Some vessels are fragile; others are strong. Each vessel has the capacity to hold something. And each vessel has a function, a purpose, for which it is designed. It is supposed to be used.

We have a lot in common with vessels. God created each of us to fulfill a different function. He wants to fill us—that's what vessels are for—with Himself through the Holy Spirit. Then He will use us to pour out His love and truth to others. God has created us to serve Him. Are we allowing Him to fill us and use us?

MATERIALS NEEDED:

A variety of vessels, such as a cup, a glass, a pot, a cake pan, a flower vase, and a trash can; water in a container; a large paper bag or a cardboard box.

INSTRUCTIONS:

Place all the containers in the bag or box. Keep the containers concealed until you mention containers found in a kitchen. At that time, take the vessels out of the bag or box and place them where everyone can see them. Hold up each vessel as you mention it. Demonstrate the capacity vessels have to hold things by pouring water from one vessel to the other. Put the vessels back in the bag or box when you have completed the object lesson.

POLLUTED VESSEL

PRINCIPLE:

It's more important to keep clean spiritually than it is to keep clean physically.

FOOD FOR THOUGHT:

Psalm 51:7,10; 1 Corinthians 3:16,17; 6:9-11; 2 Corinthians 7:1; 1 Thessalonians 4:3-7; 2 Timothy 2:20,21; Hebrews 10:22; 1 John 3:2,3

LESSON:

Today we hear a lot about pollution—pollution of the air, water, ground, environment, and even of the mind. Pollution is poison. It's dirty, even filthy; it's bad for our health.

Most of us take showers or baths regularly. We want to keep our bodies clean by washing away the pollutants and dirt that collect on them. And that's important. But it's just as important to keep ourselves clean spiritually as it is to keep ourselves clean physically—in fact, it's much *more* important! We need to be careful to keep ourselves clean from dirty thoughts and actions. It's essential that we do not let the sinful environment of the world pollute us.

MATERIALS NEEDED:

Two large bottles or cans of soft drink, two large glasses, one dirty garbage pail or trash can.

INSTRUCTIONS:

Place the soft drinks, glasses, and garbage pail or trash can in an inconspicuous place.

Emphasize the importance of keeping ourselves free from sin's pollution by presenting the following demonstration. Choose two volunteers to help you. Ceremoniously bring out your materials. Pour the contents of one soft drink bottle into a clean glass and hand it to one volunteer to drink. Then open the second bottle of soft drink. Pour it into the dirty garbage pail, swirl the soft drink around, and pour it into the second glass. Ask the other volunteer to drink the pop. When the person refuses, ask him to state the reason why he didn't want to drink it. After he says something to the effect that "It's dirty! There's no way I'd put that poison in my body! Who knows what disease it might give me!", draw an analogy to point out that in the same way, we must be careful not to pollute our spiritual selves, because that, too, can do great harm.

When you have completed the object lesson, place the soft drink containers and glasses in the garbage pail or trash can. Clean up the materials and replace them after the session.

You will need to be aware that on rare occasions, a student may attempt to drink the polluted soft drink. Don't let him or her do it! Then take advantage of the opportunity to explain that if we allow pollution in our lives, we can harm not only ourselves, but others as well.

PARASITES

PRINCIPLE:

There are people who will take all they can from a church or youth group without contributing anything in return.

FOOD FOR THOUGHT:

Matthew 7:13-23; Titus 1:10-16; James 2:14-26; Revelation 3:14-16

LESSON:

Every Christmas many people put up decorations: trees, wreaths, colored lights; we even display the Christmas cards. But watch out for the mistletoe—it's somewhere overhead (we hope!). Mistletoe adds some fun to our Christmas celebrations. But take the mistletoe out of the Christmas setting, and it is not so festive.

Mistletoe has roundish, thick green leaves and little white berries. It looks nice with a red ribbon tied around it at Christmastime. Indoors, it's fun and festive. But outdoors, where it grows, mistletoe isn't fun—it's a downright pest! It's a parasite that derives its life by feeding on living trees. We can see clusters of the plant clinging to tree branches. If there are many clusters of mistletoe drawing life from a tree, the tree will eventually die. So will the mistletoe because its source of life is gone.

When Jesus lived on earth, He walked with and spoke to multitudes of people. He taught them, healed them, and sometimes, He even provided food for them. When the people went to see Jesus, they knew they'd always receive something: a good message, the opportunity to see miracle after miracle, even great food! Many of those people were parasites. They lived off Jesus and what He could provide for them, but they didn't love Him or follow His teachings. Judas, who betrayed Jesus, was a parasite. He pretended to be a real disciple but his primary interest was money—the money he kept for Jesus and the disciples and the money he got by betraying Jesus. Judas was not part of Christ, but he lived off Him.

There are parasites in church circles, too. They are the people who say they're part of the Body but are only attending for what they can get—the freebies! These people will never be around to help when there's work to do. They don't contribute to the Body, but when a trip or great activity or a good film or a great meal has been planned, the "parasites" are there. They live off the life of the group without contributing to it.

It's hard to tell who the parasites are. Just as mistletoe looks like a healthy part of the tree at first, parasites in the group look like a healthy part of it. Often, only they themselves know that they are selfishly using the group for a time because of the fun it offers.

There will always be parasites. Be sure that you can never be called a parasite by your friends, or your pastor, or by God, who knows all things.

MATERIAL NEEDED:

Mistletoe—either real or plastic.

INSTRUCTIONS:

Place the mistletoe in your purse or pocket. Then hold it up as you describe its use at Christmastime and its parasitic characteristics. Continue to hold and refer to the mistletoe throughout the object lesson.

ALL TIED UP

PRINCIPLE:

God can free us from bad habits.

FOOD FOR THOUGHT:

Ephesians 4:22-23; 5:8-18; 6:10-17; 1 Timothy 6:9; James 1:13-15

LESSON:

We all have habits. We have good habits; we have bad habits. Good habits are necessary and helpful. Brushing our teeth is a good habit. Putting on seat belts whenever we travel in a car is a good habit. Being polite—saying "pardon me," "thank you" or "I'm sorry"—is a good habit.

On the other hand, we all have bad habits. Some have the bad habit of cursing. Others have the bad habit of always blaming others, and excusing themselves. A bad habit people seem to develop rather easily is that of putting others down or making negative comments. Arriving late to everything is another bad habit many people have.

Most of us have never thought back to the time one of our habits started. But each habit started the first time we performed the action. It was a fragile beginning, but the habit grew stronger each time we repeated the action. For example, some people started smoking because they thought it made them appear "grown-up" or macho or sophisticated. The first time they tried cigarettes, they didn't particularly like them, but smoking was the thing to do. So they kept on smoking until it became a habit, and later an addiction.

36

The process of developing habits can be illustrated with a thin strand of thread. If the thread is looped around a person's wrists once and then tied, the person has no trouble breaking the thread. If the thread is looped around the wrists four or five times before it's tied, breaking it becomes more difficult. When the thread is looped around the wrist twelve or fifteen times before it is tied, the person can't break it without hurting himself.

A habit is like the thread. At first, it is fragile—easily broken. But repetition brings strength to the habit.

How can a person with many loops of thread wrapped around his wrists be freed? It is simple—really. The person can be cut free with scissors.

A person can be freed from his bad habits, too, by asking God to break the bondage. Upon that request, God will do it. He is always eager to set free people who are caught in their bad habits. The most important part of breaking the habit—of being cut free—is the person's *desire* to be rid of the habit and his *determination* not to get caught by allowing the strands of habitual repetition to enslave him again.

MATERIALS NEEDED:

A spool of brightly colored thread and scissors.

INSTRUCTIONS:

Before the session, practice the object lesson a couple times to determine how many loops of thread it will take to immobolize a person.

Just before you begin comparing habits to thread, ask for a volunteer to assist you. Loop the thread around his wrists one time and then ask the person to try to break free. He will be able to break the thread easily. Then, loop the thread around the volunteer's wrists two or three times and ask him to try to break free. Even though it will take more effort, the person should be able to break the thread. Thank the person for his help and ask him to be seated.

Ask for another volunteer to help you. Loop the thread twelve or fifteen times around the volunteer's wrists and then knot it securely. Each time you loop the thread, talk about a bad habit. You may use conversation similar to the following: "Here's the way the habit of cursing is started." (Loop thread once around wrists.) "The person cursed one day when things didn't go his way." (Loop thread again.) "And then, a week later, he got mad and cursed again." (Loop thread again.) "And then two days later he got upset and cursed again," (add another loop), "and again," (add another loop), "and again." Continue talking and looping thread until there is enough thread around the person's wrists to keep him from breaking free easily.

Ask the person to break free. When he can't, ask if he would like to be free. When the person answers yes, cut the thread with scissors.

Then, continue with the lesson, pointing out that God is willing to set us free from bad habits when we want to be free and ask for His help.

MORE THAN MEETS THE EYE

PRINCIPLE:

God has placed great treasures in His Word for us to discover.

FOOD FOR THOUGHT:

Psalm 62:8; 112:7; 118:8; Proverbs 3:5; 16:20; John 20:29; 2 Timothy 1:12; Hebrews 10:23

LESSON:

We live in a world in which we're bombarded by commercials that make empty promises. The problem is that sometimes we believe these promises—promises that the clothes we wear will make us happy; that some deodorant, hair spray or toothpaste will make us popular; or that if we drink a certain kind of pop, we'll have a good time. When the promises are unfulfilled, we're disappointed. And pretty soon, we may become skeptical.

We often have good reason to distrust some of what we read and see and hear. But we never have to worry about placing trust in God and His Word. God has placed great treasures in the Bible, promises we can depend on God to keep, instructions for living that have our best interest in mind, words that help us know and trust God better. However, to find the treasures, we must open God's Word and study it.

MATERIALS NEEDED:

A section of a newspaper, a five or ten-dollar bill, transparent tape.

INSTRUCTIONS:

Before the session, tape the money securely in the fold of the newspaper. Fold the paper back to its original shape. Then, before anyone arrives, place the paper in an inconspicuous place, but within your reach. (It's important that no one sees you hide the paper.)

Begin discussing with the group the value we place on things, partly because of the promises we've heard about them. Then, look around and "find" your loaded paper. Casually show the paper to the group. Try to convince group members that the paper is valuable. It contains information. It may give someone an idea or reveal a secret that could be worth millions. Tell the group that you KNOW the paper has real value. Tell the group that you will give the paper to anyone who wants it. (You can be relatively sure that no one will step up to receive your "gift.") Keep trying to convince the group to trust your word until someone finally believes you and accepts the paper. Then, show the person and the group that the paper really does have value because of the money hidden in it. Conclude the object lesson by emphasizing that we can trust God and His Word. As we study the Bible, we will discover the treasures hidden in it.

A CHANCE ROLL

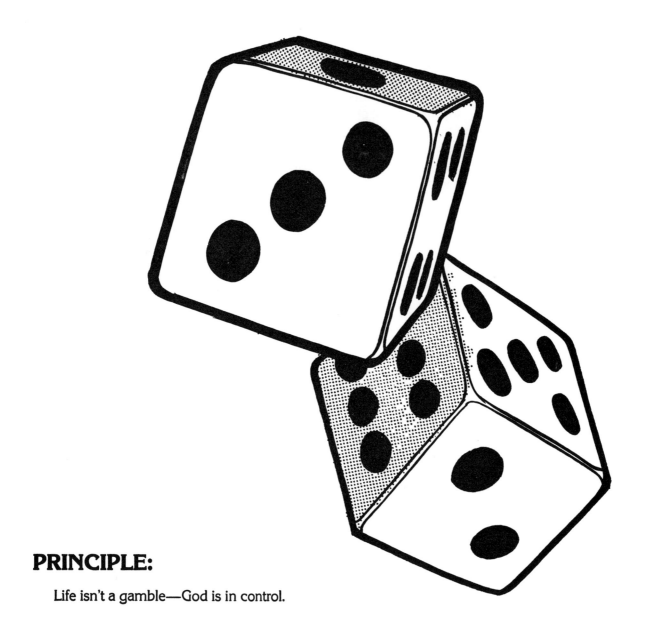

PRINCIPLE:

Life isn't a gamble—God is in control.

FOOD FOR THOUGHT:

Genesis 28:15; Psalm 139:3-16; 147:5; Proverbs 3:5,6; 16:9; Jeremiah 29:11-13; Daniel 4:17

LESSON:

Many people show, by the way they live their lives and the way they view God, that they think life is a matter of chance. To them, life is governed by no more than a divine roll of the dice. But this isn't the way God works. He doesn't gamble, He is absolute truth. He knows all things—past, present, and future. God has a plan for our lives that doesn't include chance or accident. Whether we perceive our lives unfolding by chance or by God's choice definitely affects our view of life and how we live.

MATERIALS NEEDED:

Two dice.

INSTRUCTIONS:

Place the dice in your pocket or purse. When you are ready to present the object lesson, take out the dice and let the group pass them around. Encourage the group members to interact with one another about the dice and gambling. Impress upon the students the fact that we cannot choose what numbers will come up on the dice and that gambling involves luck and chance, not choice. Then take back the dice. Use them as a visual aid while you comment about God being in control of the Christian's life.

BROKEN CONTACT

PRINCIPLE:

Sin separates us from God's power.

FOOD FOR THOUGHT:

2 Samuel 22:17-28; Isaiah 59:2; Hosea 5:4-6; 1 John 1:6,7

LESSON:

When we are in fellowship with God, we have love and joy in our lives. We feel clean. We also have the power necessary to live the Christian life as God intended us to live it. Sins separate us from that power. Even "little" things like bad attitudes, a dirty or mean thought life, or cruel words can separate us from fellowship with God. Keeping close contact with God is essential if we are to have His power in our lives.

MATERIALS NEEDED:

An extension cord, a double-pronged plug-in light socket, a 40 watt light bulb, facial tissues or plastic wrap.

42

INSTRUCTIONS:

Practice the object lesson (as described below) before the session. Arrive early so you will have time to set up before group members arrive. Plug the extension cord into an electrical outlet. Place the tissue, light bulb, and plug-in light socket out of sight. In the middle of your talk about fellowship with God and how sin breaks our contact with Him, plug in the light socket and screw the light bulb into it. The light will shine. Demonstrate broken contact (hindered fellowship) by unscrewing the light bulb and taking it out of the socket. *Unplug the extension cord.* Show the group the tissue or plastic wrap. Then place a small piece of tissue or plastic wrap over the contact in the bottom of the light socket. Ask the group if they think such a thin piece of material will keep the light bulb from shining. (Many will say no.) Screw the light bulb back into the socket *very lightly* and plug in the extension cord. The light won't shine. The object lesson illustrates how "little" sins can break our contact with God.

THAT WAGGING TONGUE

PRINCIPLE:

The tongue can be a deadly weapon.

FOOD FOR THOUGHT:

Psalm 39:1; Proverbs 15:2,4,23; 18:21; 31:26; Isaiah 50:4; Matthew 12:34; Colossians 4:6; James 3:5-10

LESSON:

Preachers, teachers, politicians, salesmen, and you and I all use our tongues to do a lot of talking. Our tongues not only work well, they also tend to work overtime. James, in his epistle, warns that the tongue can be a destructive force. Our talk can encourage others or it can hurt and destroy them.

Our tongues look small and harmless, yet how much power there is in what we use our tongues to say and how we say it! The Bible tells us to control our tongues. A rule that will help us control our tongues is to think before we speak. We must ask ourselves, "How will what I say affect others?"

Oh, that little tongue, hidden, soft and pliable. It can do so much good! It can also cause so much heartbreak. Each of us must remember the tongue and be careful how we use it.

44

MATERIALS NEEDED:

A lamb or beef tongue (available at the meat counter of many markets), paper towels, a plastic bag, a small paper bag.

INSTRUCTIONS:

If possible, use a lamb tongue for this lesson, but if one cannot be found, buy a beef tongue and cut the tip off so it looks like a human tongue. Keep the tongue refrigerated.

At home before the session, pat the tongue dry with paper towels. Place the tongue in a plastic bag and close it securely. Put the plastic bag in the paper bag. At the beginning of the object lesson, tell the group that you have an experiment to perform. Pass around the paper bag, allowing each person to feel the object inside. Ask students to guess what is in the bag. (No peeking!) Explain that no one is to tell his or her answer or comment until everyone has had a chance to feel the object. Then ask volunteers to tell what they think is in the bag. After they have responded, take the tongue out of the bag and hold it as you talk about what God says about the tongue. Be prepared for some screams and comments such as "gross." Control the group's enthusiasm. Be sure to take the tongue with you when you leave!

RIGHT ON TARGET

PRINCIPLE:

Winners have goals.

FOOD FOR THOUGHT:

Proverbs 14:22,23; 15:22; 20:18; Ecclesiastes 7:8; Matthew 24:13; 1 Corinthians 9:24-27; Philippians 3:12-14; Hebrews 12:1,2

LESSON:

As we mature, we discover who we are and where we're going. We establish goals and objectives for our lives. Goals and objectives are part of any successful person's life. However, setting goals and objectives can be threatening; when we are aiming at a target, we can miss. We can fail! And no one wants to fail. However, if we don't have a goal or target, we can't score a hit. We can't have a success. It is thrilling to set a goal and reach it. On the other hand, when we don't reach goals, when we miss, we are disappointed and even embarrassed. People who plan for success always run the risk of failing.

For some people, the risk of missing goals seems like too great a burden, so they play life as it comes. They "fly by the seat of their pants." They are like an archer who shoots an arrow and then paints a target around it. He says, "Why, that's what I was aiming at all along!"

The Lord has a plan for each of our lives. He has a purpose, a goal, for each one of us. Life isn't a matter of going off in any direction and calling what happens a success. We must set goals even if setting them introduces the possibility of failure. We will never know the thrill of hitting the bull's-eye without the threat of missing the target.

46

MATERIALS NEEDED:

One or two darts, a colorful target, a single-edged razor blade, double-sided transparent tape, a bulletin board or other large surface in which darts will stick.

INSTRUCTIONS:

Alter the target in the following way: With the razor blade, cut a line from the center of the bull's-eye to the outer edge of the target. Place double-sided transparent tape on the back of the target.

Keep the darts and target hidden until you talk about the archer who painted a target around the arrow. Then, take out a dart and throw it at the bulletin board. (Use the second dart if the first one doesn't stick.) Carry the target to the place where the dart is stuck. Open the slit you made in the target and slip it over the dart until the dart is in the center of the target. Press the target to the bulletin board. Presto! You have a bull's-eye. Then continue with the lesson.

FOOD AND FEEDING

PURPOSE:

Spiritual food is as important as physical food.

FOOD FOR THOUGHT:

Job 23:12; Psalm 107:9; 145:15,16; Isaiah 55:2; Matthew 4:4; Luke 6:21,25; John 4:32,34; 6:27,32-35,51

LESSON:

There's no question about it—food is essential. Like breathing and drinking water, eating is vital to life. We eat to live, we eat to grow, we eat to stay healthy, and we eat to stay happy. We all have different tastes and preferences, but if we are to keep healthy, we must eat a balanced diet on a daily basis. We take care of our physical bodies by eating.

Often, we tend to forget that we are spiritual beings as well as physical beings. Because we can't see our spiritual selves, we don't feel that our spiritual lives are very important. We may not sense spiritual hunger in the same way we sense physical hunger, so the spiritual part of us is often left undernourished. But the spiritual part of us is actually more important than the physical part. Our physical bodies will die, but our spirits will go on living forever.

Food for our spirits comes from God's Word. We can feed ourselves on it at church worship services, Bible school classes, Bible studies, camps, retreats, and our own daily quiet times. Our preachers, teachers, and youth pastors or Christian education directors present us with spiritual food.

However, even though we know what's best for us, most of us like junk food! In the spiritual sense, as in a physical sense, there's a lot of junk food around: fun, games, hot music. It's just what we like. But how much lasting spiritual nutrition does it give us? The Word of God is essential food. We need to "eat" more of it.

MATERIALS NEEDED:

A nutritious home-cooked meal including meat, vegetables, potatoes, bread and milk; junk food such as a fast-food hamburger, soft drink, sugary pre-packaged dessert, and candy; two plates, two glasses, silverware, tablecloth, and folding table.

INSTRUCTIONS:

Take all the materials to your meeting. Place the nutritious meal on one plate, the junk food on the other plate. Place the plates in an inconspicuous location near where you will be presenting the object lesson. When you are ready for the object lesson, set up the table and cover it with the tablecloth. Set the table with the two plates of food, silverware and glasses into which you have poured the drinks. At appropriate times during the object lesson, refer to the plate of nutritious food or the plate of junk food.

PLUG INTO POWER!

PRINCIPLE:

God's power enables us to live as Christians should.

FOOD FOR THOUGHT:

1 Chronicles 29:12; Psalm 18:28; 29:4,11; 68:35; Acts 1:8; 17:28; 1 Corinthians 6:17; Ephesians 1:19; 6:10; Philippians 4:13; Colossians 1:11

LESSON:

Power seems to be important to us today. We drive powerful cars and motorcycles. We have rockets powerful enough to launch men and women into space. Power is energy. Everything that moves, goes, works, drives, or heats requires energy.

Your Christian life was designed to run on God's power. Yet many people try to live their Christian lives without God's power.

Trying to be productive Christians without plugging into God's power is like trying to toast bread in an unplugged toaster. Kitchen appliances such as a toaster, blender and can-opener are usable only when they're plugged into a source of power. As Christians, we are usable only when we are plugged in to God's power. Plugging in means that we take time each day to meet with God, read His Word, and pray. Trying to live our Christian lives without His power is not possible. It doesn't work.

MATERIALS NEEDED:

Several small kitchen appliances such as a toaster, blender and can-opener; if necessary, an extension cord.

INSTRUCTIONS:

Conceal the appliances until you begin talking about the similarities between appliances and Christians. Then, bring out the appliances and plug one of them into an outlet or the extension cord. Turn the appliance on and off to demonstrate how it runs when it's plugged in. As you continue the talk, hold and refer to one of the appliances.

PAST THE POWER POINT

PRINCIPLE:

We lose power when we get out of touch with its source, Jesus Christ.

FOOD FOR THOUGHT:

Psalm 36:9; John 1:3,4; Acts 17:28; 1 Corinthians 6:17; James 4:8; 1 John 1:5-7

LESSON:

The Lord asks us, as He asked His first disciples, to follow Him. We can have problems when we follow Jesus, but we have even greater problems if we try to get ahead of Him.

Many of us have had the experience of growing impatient when it seems that our prayers are unanswered. God just doesn't seem to move fast enough for us. So, we may decide to take the lead. We get ahead of the source of power and guidance in our lives when we decide that we're going to take the lead away from God.

Sometimes we want God's power and presence in our lives *and* we want to hang on to some personal sins we enjoy. We stretch toward our sins, and that pulls the plug on God's power in our lives. Without His power, we're in trouble. We can go only as far as His will reaches and still enjoy His power. We must not pull against God's will. It will only result in power failure.

MATERIALS NEEDED:

An extension cord, a plug-in light socket, a light bulb.

INSTRUCTIONS:

Before the session, plug the light socket into the extension cord. Screw the light bulb into the socket. Conceal the equipment until you present the object lesson. Just before you begin to talk about stretching beyond our source of power in God, plug the extension cord into an electrical outlet. Show the group the brightly shining light bulb. Then, holding the extension cord tightly, walk away from the outlet until the plug pulls out. Repeat the procedure, demonstrating the limit of the power. This demonstration should give your students a clear visual image of what it means to walk past our source of power in Christ.

NEW BIRTH OR STILLBIRTH?

PRINCIPLE:

Spiritual growth is proof of our new life in Christ.

FOOD FOR THOUGHT:

Matthew 7:21; John 3:3-6; Romans 6:4; 8:6-14; 1 John 3:9,10,14

LESSON:

We were all born into this world. When we came into it, we were little, wrinkled, fragile, and let's face it, ugly! Despite all that, birth is a miracle.

A birth certificate certifies or gives legal proof that a baby was born. It tells when and where he was born, who his parents are, how much he weighed, and how long he was. Some birth certificates even show the baby's footprint.

Even though you can't tell it by looking at a newborn baby, or even at his birth certificate, he already has characteristics of his parents. As he grows, at least some of those characteristics will become apparent. Over the years of his life, his parents will have a great effect on him.

Ultimately, there will be another certificate made out for the baby named on the birth certificate—a death certificate. The ultimate statistic is that every person born will one day die. That is a one-to-one ratio and it is conclusive. A death certificate gives legal proof that a person has died. It tells the person's name, age, date of death and cause of death.

Birth—the start of life, and death—the end of life. Only God knows the span of the time between the beginning and the end.

As Christians, we are spiritually born again into God's family. Spiritual birth is just as real as physical birth, just as much of a miracle. When we are born into God's family, we are like little babies. We are fragile. We are hungry. And, we are a little dumb. As we feed on God's Word, we grow. We crawl, and toddle, and stumble, and learn to walk. Most important of all, as we grow, we begin to show characteristics of our heavenly Father.

A newborn Christian is alive and growing. He may make mistakes, but at least he is growing. Some people think they are newborn, or born again, into God's family, when they are really stillborn. They have an experience that seems to be a spiritual birth, and they have a form of religion, but there ends the comparison between people who are spiritually stillborn and those who are spiritually born again. Some have life. Others are dead.

It is possible for a person to go through the motions of Christianity, and yet miss a saving relationship with the Saviour. How can we tell if this happens? Simple. A newborn Christian has life. He moves, struggles, grows, even doubts from time to time. A stillborn religious person is dead from the start. His heart is cold and dead. He experiences no real growth. He is happy and content to be spiritually dead. He may even profess Christ as Saviour, but he never possesses Him as Saviour and Lord.

New birth or stillbirth. Which will it be?

54

MATERIALS NEEDED:

A birth certificate and a death certificate.

INSTRUCTIONS:

Make several copies of each certificate. As you begin talking about birth certificates, pass around the birth certificate copies for the group to examine. Repeat the procedure when you talk about the death certificate. As you start making the spiritual application, hold the original certificates in your hands and refer to them often.

BABY TALK

PRINCIPLE:

Our values and interests change as we mature.

FOOD FOR THOUGHT:

1 Corinthians 3:1-3; 13:11; Ephesians 4:14,15; Hebrews 5:12-14; 1 Peter 2:2,3

LESSON:

All of us have had toys which were valuable to us at one time. The things we value can reveal a lot about our maturity level—little babies love pacifiers, adults may "play" with cars or fashions.

As we grow, we drop childish toys and look for toys or interests more fitting to our age. Paul puts it so simply. "When I was a child, I talked like a child, I thought like a child, I reasoned like a child. When I became a man, I put childish ways behind me" (1 Cor. 13:11). Paul was telling us to grow up—but he was talking about spiritual growth.

Just as an adult who uses a pacifier or rides a tricycle is considered a tragic example of retarded maturity, so a person who has been a Christian for a long time yet hasn't grown spiritually is also to be pitied.

The interests of a truly mature Christian center on the eternal things—the things of lasting value: love, faith, bearing fruit for God, and so on. Above all else, we must love God and value our relationship with Him. That is the mark of maturity.

Most of us are into toys—real cars, clothing, records, and money! In and of themselves, toys aren't bad. But when we allow our toys to become the priority in our lives, we run the risk of allowing them to take the place of God's divine love for us and our love for Him. When we really start to mature, when we begin to grow spiritually, we will give God His rightful position and the priority in our lives that He deserves.

As we look closely at what we value, we are able to determine our level of maturity.

MATERIALS NEEDED:

Toys, such as a pacifier, baby rattle, ball, toy car, doll, tricycle, action figures; magazine pictures of an expensive sports car, well-dressed, good-looking, young man and woman; a twenty-dollar bill.

INSTRUCTIONS:

Plan how you will get the toys and pictures to the meeting. Keep them concealed until you use them in the object lesson.

As you talk about how toys show the maturity level of the user, display the toys and pictures you brought, going from those young children would enjoy to those older people would enjoy. Talk about the toys, asking questions such as "Who would find this (rattle) valuable?" Then continue with the object lesson.

RECHARGEABLE

PRINCIPLE:

We all need to spend time with God every day.

FOOD FOR THOUGHT:

Psalm 37:3-7; 63:1-8; 68:35; 91:1; 119:97-107; 121:2; Mark 1:35; Colossians 1:10,11; 1 Thessalonians 5:17

LESSON:

Healthy Christians are like a rechargeable battery. We have the capacity to receive, hold, and share spiritual power. But we aren't the source of the spiritual power. We can't generate the power on our own. We need regular "recharging." Our recharging comes from daily time alone with God.

Does getting spiritually recharged cost? Of course! Power of any kind costs. God's power costs our time. It's hard to spend time with God on a consistent basis. But it's worth the investment. We'll keep our spiritual charge!

MATERIALS NEEDED:

One regular and one rechargeable battery that look alike; a battery charger.

INSTRUCTIONS:

Conceal the batteries and battery charger until you present the object lesson. Introduce the object lesson by showing the batteries to the group and explaining the difference between them. You may use conversation similar to the following: "I'm holding two batteries. They look alike. But they're different. What do you think the difference is?" (Pause. Give students an opportunity to answer.) "One is a standard battery. It's a good battery, and it works well. But it's a one shot deal. You use it until it's dead and then you throw it away. The other battery is rechargeable. It costs more than a regular battery. But because this battery can be recharged with a battery charger like this one, the battery can be used again and again."

As you speak, hold up or point to the appropriate battery or the battery charger. Conclude the object lesson by comparing healthy Christians to the rechargeable battery as outlined in the lesson.

GIFT PACKAGE

PRINCIPLE:

In order to be a gift, what is offered must be received.

FOOD FOR THOUGHT:

Matthew 7:11; Romans 5:17; 6:23; 8:32; Ephesians 2:8; James 1:17

LESSON:

We all like gifts. We've liked them since we were small. Many of us feel that one of the best days of the year is our birthday. That's when we expect to receive gifts. That's *our* gift day.

A gift is a free expression of love—it can't be earned or purchased. But in order for a gift truly to be a gift, it must be accepted. When we offer a gift to someone and he takes it, it's a gift. There are no more conditions.

God calls the gospel a gift. It is the free gift of God. However, many people won't receive or accept the gift. God is holding out His gift of eternal life. Accepting it is our move.

MATERIALS NEEDED:

One nicely wrapped gift box with a five-dollar bill inside.

INSTRUCTIONS:

Emphasize the fact that in order to be a gift, the gift must be received, by offering the gift box to a member of the group. You may use conversation such as, "Here's a gift. See how nicely it's wrapped. None of you knows what's inside though, or for that matter, you don't really know if anything is inside. How many of you think there is anything valuable inside? This could be a joke, right? Would any of you like this gift?" Give the gift to someone, commenting that now, the gift is his. Then continue with the lesson.

MONKEY TRAP

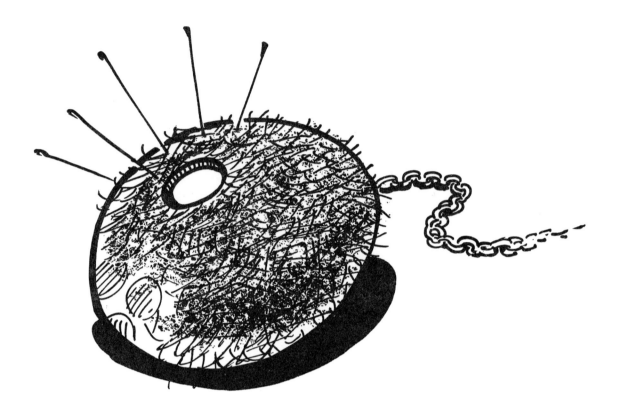

PRINCIPLE:

Satan sets traps for us by offering us good things; however, he offers them at the wrong time, in the wrong place, or for the wrong purposes.

FOOD FOR THOUGHT:

Proverbs 1:10,19; 15:27; Luke 12:15; 1 Corinthians 10:12,13; 2 Corinthians 2:11; Ephesians 6:11-13; 1 Timothy 4:1; 6:9,10; James 1:12-15; 1 Peter 5:8,9

LESSON:

The most popular animals at the zoo are the monkeys. Many people can stand for hours, watching and laughing at their silly antics. As you've watched the monkeys in a zoo, have you ever wondered how they got there? Some of them were born in the zoo or transferred there from other zoos. But some of them were trapped, captured, and then brought to the zoo.

One way to catch monkeys is by using a monkey trap. It's just a coconut shell with a small hole drilled in one side. A small, strong chain is attached to one end. It's an innocent little device that works every time. This simple trap is so effective because monkeys are curious, greedy, and stubborn. (That sounds a lot like people!)

A monkey trapper carefully fastens the chain of the trap to a small tree. Then, when he is sure a group of monkeys is watching, the trapper drops bait, such as glittering glass baubles, into the hole in the trap. When the trapper moves out of sight, monkeys come to investigate the trap. Ultimately, one monkey reaches into the hole to grab the bait. But the monkey can't get its hand out of the coconut. When the monkey grabbed the bait, it formed a fist. And the fist won't fit through the hole. The greedy little monkey doesn't want to let go of the glass baubles; another monkey might get them! But the monkey can't enjoy its new treasure. When the monkey tries to walk away with the coconut, the chain pulls tight. The monkey is trapped.

If the monkey would let go of the glass beads, the monkey could pull its fist out of the coconut and go free. But as long as the monkey holds the bait in its hand, the monkey trap has worked. The monkey trapper throws a net over the monkey and takes it away from the forest.

Satan is a master trapper, and he sets traps, similar to a monkey trap, for us. He often baits the trap with things that at a different time, or under different conditions, or in another place, would be good. The Christian, tempted by the bait, gets caught when he or she grasps it.

It's important to know that if we find we've been caught in one of Satan's traps, we can ask God to help set us free. Then our part is to know that the strength of the trap isn't in the coconut, or the tree, or the chain but rather in ourselves. The trap holds us only as long as we hold onto the bait! When we let go of Satan's bait and wait for God to give us our desires in His time, we have the freedom to enjoy the good things He gives.

MATERIALS NEEDED:

One dried coconut, shiny pieces of glass or glass beads, small sturdy chain, short length of wire, knife or screwdriver, wood file, drill and drill bit.

INSTRUCTIONS:

Cut the husk off the coconut. Bore a small hole, about 2-½ inches in diameter, in one side of the coconut. (If necessary, use a file to enlarge the drill bit hole.) Allow the coconut meat to dry for several days. Then chip out the meat with a knife or screwdriver. (The coconut meat tastes great!) File the hole smooth. Wire the chain to one end of the coconut.

Hold and refer to the trap throughout the object lesson. Save the trap for future use.

MIRROR, MIRROR, ON THE WALL

PRINCIPLE:

God's Word is like a mirror: it shows us what we need to do but it doesn't do it for us.

FOOD FOR THOUGHT:

Psalm 1:2; 119:48,97-107; 2 Timothy 2:15; James 1:21-25

LESSON:

The first thing many of us did this morning after we jumped out of bed was to look at ourselves in the mirror. We may not have liked what we saw, but we saw it anyway. How the truth hurts!

Most of us look at ourselves in a mirror many times a day. Why? Because we want to see if we look all right. A mirror shows us what we need to do to make ourselves presentable.

The Bible is like a spiritual mirror. It shows us what we need to do, where we need to do it, when we need to do it, and how to do it. But we're expected to take action and do it! The Bible always reflects the truth. Only a fool avoids the truth. Only a fool, when he or she knows what needs to be done, fails to do it!

MATERIAL NEEDED:

A hand mirror.

INSTRUCTIONS:

As you mention how often and why we use mirrors, hold up the mirror you brought. Explain that the book of James compares the Bible to a mirror. You may use conversation similar to the following: "The Bible shows us what we are really like. Often, we don't like what it shows us. Now, suppose you looked in the mirror in the morning and saw that you were a real mess. Then you just went to school without cleaning up or combing your hair. When your friends spotted you, they laughed and pointed to you saying, 'You look terrible!' With a smile, you replied, 'I know, I looked at myself in a mirror this morning. I do look awful!' and walked on. It's not likely that any of us would go anywhere knowing we were a total mess. But often we may read something in the Bible and think *I really fall short of this instruction* and do nothing about it. How often do you follow through by straightening up the spiritual messes the Bible shows us?"

Conclude the object lesson by making further comparisons between a mirror and the Bible as outlined in the lesson.

GARBAGE!!

PRINCIPLE:

Satan presents us with nice gift packages, but there's garbage inside them.

FOOD FOR THOUGHT:

Psalm 62:10; Proverbs 11:3,4; 16:25; 27:6; Romans 6:20-23; 16:18; Ephesians 4:22; 1 Timothy 6:9,10; James 1:14,15; 2 Peter 2:18-20

LESSON:

Packaging is a big thing today. The products we buy are packaged to make them look expensive, bigger than life, and colorful! The manufacturer wants to make the product appealing—irresistible.

From time to time, we do a little "packaging" of our own. We wrap gifts so that they look appealing and pretty on the outside without giving away what's on the inside. And oh, how provocative those packages can be! At Christmas, as the packages begin to pile up under the tree, we take special interest in them. Which ones are ours? What do they sound like when we shake them? Are they big? Heavy? Perhaps we even try to guess what's inside.

The truth is, we can't tell the value of a gift by the way it's wrapped. God has given us the gifts of His promises and eternal life. Those are precious, valuable gifts, but they don't necessarily come in bright, flashy packages.

Satan, the father of lies and deception, makes promises, too. However, Satan majors on the gift wrapping rather than the contents. Foolish people that we are, we rush to unwrap the beautiful packages, only to find disappointment inside—stinking garbage! Too bad, it comes in such nice packages!

Before we get too thrilled about what Satan offers us, we'd better check inside. A fast life, lots of fun, sex and money, money, money make attractive packages. But what's inside? Pull off the paper and packaging Satan has so cleverly used, and we find neatly curled inside a deadly snake whose mission is to promote sin and death (see Rom. 6:23).

Who wants garbage? Who would send us garbage as a gift? We'd better check our gift over before we accept it. Better yet—we'd better check out the one who is giving it to us.

MATERIALS NEEDED:

Two gift boxes, one large and one small, two different kinds of gift wrap and ribbon; scissors; transparent tape; a small, nice gift or a five-dollar bill; "ripe" garbage; zip-lock bag or plastic wrap; large paper sack.

INSTRUCTIONS:

Place the gift or money in the small box. Wrap it carelessly, tying the ribbon off center and leaving tape sticking out from the edges. Place the garbage in a zip-lock bag or wrap it securely in plastic wrap. Place the garbage in the large box. (The garbage won't smell or leak, but it will make the box feel heavy.) Wrap the box carefully and extravagantly, making it lovely to look at. Place the two packages in the large paper sack to conceal them until it's time for the object lesson.

Take the gifts from the sack as you talk about gifts. You may say something like, "I've brought two packages with me. As you can see, one is rather small and the other one is large. There's something in each of these packages. I'm going to pass the packages around. You try to tell me which one is of greater value. If given a choice, which one would you take?" Allow time for the packages to be passed around, for the group members to speculate about the value of the packages, and for students to decide which gift they would be most likely to choose. (You may allow two students to choose packages to keep. If so, instruct each student to open the package as you talk about it.)

Explain that you can't tell the value of a gift by the way it's wrapped. Then slowly unwrap the small gift as you talk about God's gifts.

Then begin to open the large package. Pace yourself so that your comments about garbage will coincide with the revealing of the package contents.

WALKING SHOES

PRINCIPLE:

Learning to walk with God, like learning to walk as a child, has its ups and downs.

FOOD FOR THOUGHT:

Psalm 18:36; 23:3,4; 37:23,24; 119:45,133; Proverbs 3:23; 4:17,19,26; 16:19; Isaiah 40:31; Micah 4:5; 6:8; Galatians 5:25; 1 John 2:6

LESSON:

Learning to walk as a toddler and learning to walk spiritually are very much the same. As babies, we took a lot of tumbles before walking became second nature to us. And as Christians, we experience many ups and downs before it seems natural to walk in the ways God wants us to walk. But we must keep trying. That's the only way to learn to walk. When we were babies learning to walk, we fell often. But our mothers didn't punish us or call us names because we fell. They gently pulled us up and encouraged us to try again because they wanted us to learn to walk. And they knew we could. God is just the same: He helps us learn to walk. He encourages us.

There's another interesting point about learning to walk. When we fell as babies, it usually didn't hurt much because we were close to the floor. We didn't fall very far. As babies, we were better equipped for falling than we are now. If we take a fall now, it hurts. Take a fall when we're eighty and it will really hurt. Why? Because the older we get, the more our bodies are adjusted to standing and walking—not falling!

As we mature and grow as Christians, we must not get discouraged when we fall—we must keep trying to walk. Learning to be upright in our Christian lives isn't always easy—but it's great to be able to follow Christ with fewer and fewer falls.

MATERIALS NEEDED:

Several pairs of shoes; booties or baby shoes, shoes for a nine-or ten-year-old, shoes for an adult; a bag or box.

INSTRUCTIONS:

Conceal the shoes in a box or bag and take the shoes to your session. At the beginning of the object lesson, show the shoes. Use conversation similar to the following as you talk about the shoes.

"Look at these shoes. What do they remind you of? Stinky feet? Maybe! But they remind us of two other things. First, because they are of different types and sizes, they remind us of growth—of different stages of our lives. Second, they remind us of walking. Primarily, shoes are to help us walk more comfortably.

"When we were babies, we wore cute little shoes like these booties. Then, we started wearing little shoes like these. And the difference in these two pairs of shoes marked a big advancement in our lives—we learned to walk!

"Learning to walk was hard—it had lots of ups and downs. Learning to walk might have happened something like this: One day your mom stood you by the couch. You held on as you watched her walk a few steps away, hold out her arms and call you to her. You took one or two steps toward her, and then you fell. You sat there with an astounded look on your face. Your mom picked you up, put you by the couch again—and you repeated the entire process. Up and down. Up and down. Over and over again, you practiced walking until it became natural to you. When you fell, you didn't just sit there and insist you would never walk again; that you had tried and failed so many times you would never learn to walk. You kept trying. And you've been running or walking ever since."

Conclude the object lesson by comparing learning to walk as a baby with learning to walk spiritually.

TOOLS

PRINCIPLE:

There are tools which can help us study the Bible more effectively.

FOOD FOR THOUGHT:

Psalm 1:2; 119:48,97-107; Proverbs 4:7; 19:2; 24:3,4; 2 Timothy 2:15

LESSON:

Every day, we use tools that helps us in many different ways. Pencils and pens help us write clearly. Wrenches and screwdrivers and pliers make it possible for us to do a hundred different tasks we can't do with our bare hands.

There are tools available to help us better understand and study God's Word, too. Of course, these tools look a lot different from a set of wrenches or a knife. But they definitely help us to be more effective in our study of God's Word.

A Bible handbook is a great little tool. It gives a brief history of the Bible, an overview of each book of the Bible, and maps of countries and empires as they existed in Bible times. Some Bible handbooks also give us helpful insights into the customs of Bible people; lists of dates, events, and important people; and historical background. There's a great deal of important information packed into one of these little tools.

A concordance is another good Bible study tool. It makes it possible to locate a Bible verse—fast. Suppose we knew just one or two words from a Bible verse. Instead of reading the Bible from the beginning until we found the verse, we'd look up the word in the concordance. Then we'd look up the references listed in the concordance and read those verses until we found the verse we were looking for.

Bible commentaries help us understand difficult passages. When we find a hard-to-understand passage, we can refer to a commentary and read how the Bible experts explain the meaning of the passage. Bible commentaries also can give us deeper understanding or new insights into Bible passages we already understand.

Using tools to help us better understand and apply God's Word can make a real difference in our understanding of God and His Word and our Christian growth.

MATERIALS NEEDED:

Various automotive and household tools, Bible handbook, one or two Bible commentaries, a Bible concordance, any other books which you feel will help your students in their study of the Bible, a large sheet or table cloth, a table.

INSTRUCTIONS:

Arrive well before the session is to begin. Place the tools and books on the table. Cover them with the sheet or cloth.

At the beginning of the object lesson, uncover the tools. As you introduce the object lesson, use conversation similar to this: "It isn't hard to guess what these are; they're tools. There seem to be as many tools as there are jobs to do."

Discuss some specific ways in which the tools you brought can be used. Then, present the Bible study tools you brought and talk about ways they can be used.

ABIDING IN CHRIST

PRINCIPLE:

We find strength and spiritual health by abiding in Christ.

FOOD FOR THOUGHT:

Jeremiah 29:12-14; John 8:31; 14:19,20; 15:1-8; 1 Corinthians 6:15,17; Philippians 3:9; 1 John 2:24; 4:13

LESSON:

Jesus Christ is concerned about our relationship with Him. In John 15, Jesus explained that He is like a grapevine, and each of His followers are like the branches that come from the vine.

If we look closely at a grapevine, we see many small branches coming from it. Without the vine, the branches cannot exist. If a branch is cut from the vine, it loses its resilience; it becomes brittle and dies. However, when the branch is connected to the vine it receives nourishment from the vine. Then the branch produces fruit. As long as the branch is connected to the vine, the branch is abiding in the vine.

Jesus used the illustration of the vine and branches because it clearly represents the relationship we have with Him. As long as we are abiding in Christ, He is able to give us spiritual strength and health. Abiding in Christ means spending time in close relationship with Him. Spending time with Christ each day through prayer and Bible study are essential for spiritual nourishment, growth, and the production of fruit in our lives. Being connected to Christ—abiding in Christ—is our strength and health.

MATERIALS NEEDED:

A grapevine with branches, or a small tree or shrub limb with branches.

INSTRUCTIONS:

Arrive early and place the branch where it can't be easily seen, but where it will be easy to reach.

Show the vine or limb to the group as you begin talking about the vine and branches. If you could not find a grapevine, explain that the limb illustrates the same principle. Refer to the vine or branch often during the object lesson, pointing out the place where the branches connect.

POSITION!

PRINCIPLE:

God is the one who positions us in His Body.

FOOD FOR THOUGHT:

John 15:5; Romans 12:4-8; 1 Corinthians 12:14-31; Ephesians 4:25

LESSON:

Everywhere we look, people have positions. Some people have titles. Some have big offices and some have little offices and some have no offices at all. At school, there is the custodian, the teacher, the vice-principal, and the principal. From the bottom to the top—right up the ladder.

Sometimes we look at all the positions in the world and think that the same sort of positions should apply to the Christian life. That's when pride, ambition, and politics enter the Christian community.

John 15 tells us that Jesus talked about the Christian's position. Jesus said that He is the vine— the grapevine—and His followers are the branches. The vine dictates the position of the branches. A new little branch that's getting ready to sprout doesn't say to the vine, "I want to grow at the top," or, "I want to grow right here in the center," or, "Let me grow near the bottom." The vine pops out the new little branch in just the right place so it can function in it's proper way.

Let's not be too eager to push ourselves into position in the Body of Christ. So often we would like to be somewhere else, doing someone else's job, or having someone else's responsibility. God knows where we should be. He has a place for us. His place! We will be able to function best in that special place in the vine.

74

MATERIALS NEEDED:

A grapevine with branches or a small tree or shrub limb with branches.

INSTRUCTIONS:

Arrive early enough so that you can conceal the vine or branch before group members arrive. Place the branch where it won't be easily seen but where it will be easily accessible.

Hold the vine or limb and point to the branches as you talk about their position.

THE CANARY CAGE

PRINCIPLE:

Although we may feel that God's laws restrict us, in fact, they protect us.

FOOD FOR THOUGHT:

Psalm 119:71; Isaiah 55:8; Matthew 7:13,14; Romans 13:1-5; Hebrews 12:5-11

LESSON:

A domestic bird's world is a small one because it lives in a cage. It would be a drag for us to live in such a restricted environment. But a domestic bird seems to adjust pretty well. It seems happy. It has everything it needs: food, water, shelter. But what does a little bird think of as it looks through the bars of the cage? Does it want freedom? Does it want to scratch around outside with the other birds? We don't know what the bird thinks or feels, but we do know this: If the cage door were to be left open and the bird got outdoors, it would fly away. The sad fact is that the domestic bird would not be able to survive that sort of freedom. It would starve, or be killed by other birds or animals. The bird escaping the cage is in reality abandoning its protection.

We can easily understand that the bird is safer in its cage than it is outdoors—whether the bird knows it or not. But what can we learn from this example?

Let's take a look at ourselves. Sometimes rules seem to restrict us like the bars of a cage. All those rules seem to be made to keep us from having fun and enjoying ourselves. They seem to take away our freedom! Yet we realize, when we really stop to think about it, that rules are necessary to protect both ourselves and our society.

God, too, has given us rules. We can obey them—and some people call that restriction. Or we can break them—which is irresponsible freedom. God has given us His rules for our own good so that we can live long, productive lives. If we violate His divine laws, like the little domestic bird which flies away from its cage, we ultimately destroy ourselves. Our freedom is really a matter of where we are and how we view our position in relationship to God.

MATERIALS NEEDED:

A small domestic bird, such as a parakeet or canary, in a bird cage.

INSTRUCTIONS:

As you talk, refer to the bird in its cage. If possible, hold the cage and/or the bird as you give the object lesson.

OVER THE LINE

PRINCIPLE:

God demands that we stand with Him.

FOOD FOR THOUGHT:

1 Kings 18:21; Matthew 6:24; 12:30; James 1:6-8; 1 Peter 3:15; Revelation 3:15,16

LESSON:

Lines are everywhere! There are lines in parking lots to designate the parking spaces. There are lines drawn at intersections so that pedestrians know where to cross the street. There are little, but important, lines drawn on rulers to show units of measure. There are lines drawn on baseball diamonds, basketball courts, and football fields to help the players and referees know if the balls, and players, are in or out.

Lines can be very important. They help us know where we stand. We're either on one side of the line or the other.

Exodus 32 tells us that Moses drew a line. Here's why: God's people had participated in a drunken party and had worshiped a golden calf. Drunken idolaters! Moses knew that God demands that people love, obey, and worship only Him. In a very courageous move, Moses stepped in front of all those people and drew a line by saying, "Whoever is for the Lord, come to me" (Exod. 32:26). That day, many people crossed the line by standing with Moses and the Lord.

Jesus, too, drew a line when He called those from the multitude to follow Him. Jesus' words make a very clear line: either you are for Christ or you are against Him. That same line exists today. An important line. We must decide on which side of that line we will stand.

MATERIALS NEEDED:

One-half or three-quarter inch wide white or light-colored adhesive tape.

INSTRUCTIONS:

Cut an eight-foot (2.4-m) length of adhesive tape and place it in a straight line on the floor.

When you explain that lines help us know which side we are on, ask the group to stand and look at the line. Then instruct half of the group to stand on one side of the line while the other half stands on the other side. Explain that the group is now divided by the line. Then ask one group member to move from one side of the line to the other. As he does so, point out that the person has crossed the line. He knows exactly on which side of the line he stands. Then ask all group members to return to their seats. Continue your talk about the importance of taking a stand on God's side.

THE FOUNDATION

PRINCIPLE:

A Christian should build his or her life on the foundation of God's Word.

FOOD FOR THOUGHT:

Psalm 127:1; Isaiah 28:16; Matthew 7:24-27; Luke 6:47-49; 1 Corinthians 3:11; Colossians 2:7; 1 Timothy 6:19

LESSON:

Sand is easy to move. Wind blows it away and rain washes it away. Sand is ever changing and shifting.

Rock, on the other hand, is hard and solid. It is permanent. Lasting. Sand and rock are different. Sand is temporary; rock is permanent.

We can read in Matthew 7 some things Jesus had to say about sand and rock. He compared sand and rock as foundations to build on. Jesus said, "Everyone who hears these words of mine and puts them into practice is like a wise man who built his house on the rock. The rain came down, the streams rose, and the winds blew and beat against that house; yet it did not fall, because it had its foundation on rock. But everyone who hears these words of mine and does not put them into practice is like a foolish man who built his house on sand. The rain came down, the streams rose, and the winds blew and beat against that house, and it fell with a great crash" (Matt. 7:24-27).

A building must be built on a strong foundation if it is to stand through storms and years of use. In the same way, we must build our lives on a firm foundation if we expect to withstand life's struggles, hard times, and temptations. We can build on a firm foundation if we follow Jesus' teaching. First we must locate the rock—which is truth. And then we must build our foundation on that rock.

Building the foundation for our lives is hard work. In our hurry-up, instant world, we may not want to take the time to build a solid foundation. We'd rather get on with building our lives. But without a solid foundation, the lives we build have nothing to hold them up.

We need to take time to build solid foundations. Otherwise, we are like the person Jesus called a fool. That person had heard the Word—the truth—but he didn't act on it. He didn't see the need to build his house on the solid rock foundation. So, he built his house on sand. We run the risk of building on sand, too, if we build our lives on popularity, sports, a house, a car, a romantic relationship, a job, money—or a hundred other things. All these things are temporary—they're sand. When the storms come, the wind and water will wash away the sand we've built on and our lives will fall, as Jesus said the foolish man's house fell, with a great crash!

In the story Jesus told, a storm hit the house of the man who built on the rock. Even when we build on the solid rock foundation of God's Word, we will experience storms. God never promised

Christians that they would always have blue skies. We will have our share of storms. But if we've built on the solid foundation, our lives won't blow apart like the foolish man's; we will be able to ride out the storms.

We must be sure to be like the wise man, building our foundations on the Word of God. Foundation building is important. We must dig deep, sweat, and work hard. We won't be sorry we did.

MATERIALS NEEDED:

A large, clear plastic sack with sand in it; a large rock.

INSTRUCTIONS:

Show the sand and the rock at the beginning of the object lesson. Then refer to them at appropriate times as you talk about building on a firm foundation.

CONFORMED

PRINCIPLE:

We are not to be conformed to this world.

FOOD FOR THOUGHT:

2 Kings 17:15; Romans 1:21-23; 12:2; 2 Corinthians 3:18; Hebrews 6:12; 1 Peter 1:14-16; 1 John 3:2,3

LESSON:

In the book of Romans, Paul says, "Do not conform any longer to the pattern of this world, but be transformed by the renewing of your mind" (Rom. 12:2). Paul is telling us that even though we're living in the world, we are to be different. We are not to take on the world's pattern. We are not to become like other people living in the world.

Unfortunately, many Christians are taking on the world's pattern. Under pressure, their values have changed. Their loyalties have changed. Their testimonies have changed. Like a piece of foil pressed over a penny, they have taken on the image of the world.

We aren't to conform to the world. Instead we are to be transformed by the renewing of our minds. "Transform" means to change the makeup of something or to change its structure. Quite different from conforming—adapting ourselves to prevailing standards and customs. Conforming is a worldly process. Transforming is the work we allow the Holy Spirit to do in our lives. It's our choice—conformed or transformed.

MATERIALS NEEDED:

Aluminum foil, several coins.

INSTRUCTIONS:

Cut aluminum foil into 3x3-inch (7.5x7.5-cm) squares. (Make 20 percent more squares than the number of people you anticipate to be in the group.) Before the session, practice pressing the foil over the coin (see instructions below) so you will be confident as you lead the group.

After you briefly discuss Romans 12:2, ask the group to define the word "conform." After volunteers respond, ask each person to take out a coin. (If some students do not have coins, let them use the ones you brought.) Then give each person a square of aluminum foil. Guide the group in conforming the foil to the coin by using conversation similar to the following: "Let's demonstrate what it is to be conformed. Place the coin on a hard surface. Now, take the foil and place it over the center of the coin. Press hard on top of the foil so that it is pressed down around the image on the coin. Keep pressing until the image on the coin is visible through the foil. Now, gently take the foil off the coin and presto! Your foil has taken on the appearance of the coin. You have conformed the foil to the coin. Note that your foil is not part of the coin. It isn't the same. It does not have the same value. It simply has been conformed—or made to look like—the coin."

After you have clearly defined "conformed" by using the foil and coins, continue the lesson by talking about how some Christians are conformed to the world.

FORGET THE INSTRUCTIONS!

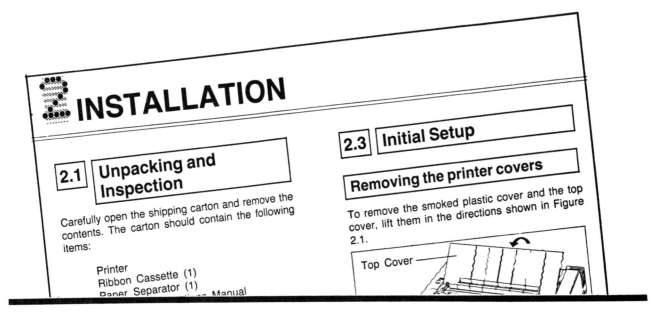

PRINCIPLE:

God is qualified to give us instructions.

FOOD FOR THOUGHT:

Psalm 1:1,2; 16:7,8,11; 32:8; 119:133; Isaiah 55:11,12; Colossians 1:9; 2:3; 2 Peter 3:18

LESSON:

There are many situations in which people receive instruction. Teachers instruct their pupils. Parents instruct their children. Pastors instruct their congregations. Even with so much instruction available, many of us tend to take it lightly.

Almost all of us at one time or another have been so eager to work on a project or to build something that we've dived right in without reading the instructions. We think we know how it works! Who needs the instructions? Soon, we have an extra part or something doesn't fit. *Then* we read the instructions. In the meantime, we've wasted a lot of time and effort.

Unfortunately, we do the same thing with our lives. We're so busy living that we don't take time to learn the instructions for living from the One who created us. After all, we're the best qualified to know what will make us happy and successful—right? Wrong! God knows better. He made us. He made the world. He made life. It's sensible to assume that He is qualified to give us instruction. The Bible is God's instruction manual for living. In it, we find how to live, how to be truly successful, and even how to be happy.

Our mistakes may cause us to go back and read God's instruction manual. That's good. God knows us and the world He created. Let's follow His instructions.

MATERIALS NEEDED:

Boxes or cans with instructions printed on them, an instruction sheet from a model project, a new car manual, a Bible, a table or desk.

INSTRUCTIONS:

Before the session, place the objects on the table or desk in the order in which you will refer to them. Introduce the object lesson by picking up each object and displaying it while you talk about it. You may use conversation such as, "Look. Here are some instructions printed on the back of a cake mix box. Here are some instructions for putting together a model airplane. And here is a care and instruction manual for a new car."

Then continue with the object lesson, emphasizing the importance of following the instructions God has given us in the Bible.

THERE'S A DIFFERENCE

PRINCIPLE:

God holds us responsible for our actions.

FOOD FOR THOUGHT:

Matthew 12:36; Luke 12:48; Romans 14:10-12; Hebrews 2:2,3; James 2:12,13; 1 Peter 3:15,21; 2 John 1:8

LESSON:

There are many similarities and many differences between humans and cats. For example, both cats and humans have blood which is pumped by a heart. Both cats and humans can hear, see, and smell. Like cats, humans can be angered. Both can feel fear. Both can be hungry and thirsty. Humans and cats are similar. But they are different, too. Most people don't have fur all over their bodies. They don't walk on four legs, and most of them don't prefer mice for dinner!

One major difference between people and animals is that people are responsible for their actions. A cat or a dog is not responsible for his actions. A cat or dog or horse is not capable of being responsible. If a dog bites someone, the injured person doesn't take the dog to court. He takes the owner to court. If a cat scratches someone, the cat's owner is responsible. Society holds people responsible not only for the actions of their pets, but also for their own actions.

God, too, holds people responsible for their actions. God has created us to live forever—with or without Him. We are responsible for our decisions and for the consequences of those decisions. God has placed the responsibility of obeying His laws, and the consequences of disobedience, on each of us. That's why each person must make his or her own decision about his or her relationship with God and whether or not to obey His laws. The decisions we make can have eternal consequences. We are each responsible for the spiritual direction we take.

MATERIALS NEEDED:

A tame, friendly, well-fed cat; a box or carrying cage.

INSTRUCTIONS:

Be sure the cat is accustomed to you and won't be spooked by the group. Begin the object lesson by picking up the cat and introducing it to the group. You might say something like, "This is Tabby. She isn't really going to get much out of the lesson today. But I brought her to illustrate a point. We are people. This is a cat. We are humans. This is an animal."

Hold the cat as you continue to compare and contrast similarities and differences between the cat and humans. If the cat gets restless, put it in its box or cage.

FRUIT

PRINCIPLE:

Just as branches are for growing fruit, Christians who abide in Christ will bear spiritual fruit.

FOOD FOR THOUGHT:

John 15:4,5,16; Galatians 5:22,23; Ephesians 5:9; Colossians 1:10

LESSON:

Jesus said, "I am the vine; you are the branches" (John 15:5). Christians are like the branches that grow from a grapevine. Like us, each branch is unique. Some branches are long, some are short, some have more leaves than others. But there is one thing all branches on the grapevine have in common—they are all supposed to bear fruit. Bearing fruit comes *naturally* to grapevines. We never hear the grapevine telling the branches to bear fruit. The vine never threatens the branch for not bearing more fruit—the branches aren't sweating a fruit quota. Ten grapes by Thursday or else! No groaning and moaning! Fruit is the natural product of a healthy branch.

There are some other fascinating characteristics of the branches on a grapevine. First, they don't compare fruit. "Look at my nice cluster! You have just a few grapes—and some dried up raisins, too!" Second, fruit doesn't show off. Sometimes the harvesters have to look carefully to find it. Third, the branches never produce fruit for themselves—but always for others. It's a giving situation.

Jesus compared Himself to the vine and His followers to the branches. Let's take a little time to compare ourselves to the branches. Do we bear fruit naturally? Do we compare our fruit with that of others? Do we show off the fruit we bear—are we proud of it?

While we're comparing, let's consider carefully the fruit the branches produce. It grows in clusters. Each cluster is made up of many pieces of fruit. Similarly, fruit in the Christian's life isn't just evangelism, or just good works, or just godly attributes. It's all of these and more. Our lives, like the branches, are for the purpose of bearing a variety of good fruit. As we abide in Christ, our lives will naturally bear more and more good fruit.

MATERIALS NEEDED:

A cluster of grapes, a grapevine, or a tree limb with branches on it.

INSTRUCTIONS:

At the beginning of the object lesson, show the cluster of grapes and grapevine. If you don't have a grapevine, show the limb and explain that it is a substitute for the grapevine. Refer to the vine, the branches and the fruit at appropriate times throughout the object lesson.

WHAP!

PRINCIPLE:

Satan uses tantalizing bait when he sets traps for Christians.

FOOD FOR THOUGHT:

Genesis 3:1; Matthew 4:1-3; 2 Corinthians 2:11; 1 Timothy 6:9; James 1:14,15

LESSON:

Mousetraps were built to catch mice. Keeping in mind what mice are like, and using common materials—wood, wire, and metal—the inventor of the common mousetrap built a very effective device.

A mouse gets caught when it goes after the cheese baiting the trap. There's nothing wrong with the cheese. But it is the wrong time, the wrong place, and the wrong conditions for the mouse to eat the cheese. Most mice caught in traps have two things in common. One, they have a mouthful of cheese—their last bite! And, two, they're dead! Those mice were more concerned with the bait than the conditions that surrounded it.

Satan is a great inventor of very effective traps in which to catch Christians. He knows what we are like, and he can arrange simple, everyday things into a trap that will cripple us and pull us away from God's fellowship and His will. Satan is clever—he personalizes the conditions and the bait he uses when he sets traps for us. If he's after a person (and he's after all of us!) he will bait the trap with something that will attract the person; something he or she likes; and usually, something good. But he places the bait so that it is at the wrong time, in the wrong place, or under the wrong conditions. The bait may be money. Money isn't bad—we all need it. Or sex. There's nothing wrong with sex—it's how we all got here. Or friends. Most of us would have a hard time getting along without friends. But under the wrong conditions, any of these things can lead us into one of Satan's traps.

The mouse that is more concerned with the bait than the conditions that surround it is sure to get caught. Christians, too, who are more interested in the bait Satan uses than the conditions that surround it are bound to get caught in his trap. There are plenty of traps out there. Let's not get caught in them.

MATERIALS NEEDED:

A mousetrap.

INSTRUCTIONS:

Show the mousetrap at the beginning of the object lesson and snap it a couple of times to capture the group's attention. Then, as you continue the lesson, hold the mousetrap so everyone can see it.

THE PRUNING PROCESS

PRINCIPLE:

God sometimes prunes some good things out of our Christians lives in order to help us produce better fruit.

FOOD FOR THOUGHT:

Matthew 7:15-20; John 15:2; Hebrews 12:11

LESSON:

Jesus said, "I am the vine; you are the branches" (John 15:5). There are many branches on a grapevine. Each branch is there to produce good fruit and a lot of it. Each branch on a grapevine not only produces fruit, but it also produces smaller branches and leaves. The branch needs the smaller branches and leaves to survive. However, when a branch gets too bushy, all those branches and leaves affect the branch's fruit-producing capability. The small branches and leaves use up the nutrients that would normally go to the fruit. The bushier the branch becomes, the fewer and smaller the grapes become. The farmer prunes away the unnecessary smaller branches and leaves so that the branch can produce better fruit.

God prunes us in the same way a farmer prunes the branches on his grapevines. Often, our lives become bushy—full of good activities and programs, good ideas and plans. But when all that "bushiness" gets in the way of our producing good fruit, God begins to prune us. He trims away our bushiness. Sometimes we don't understand what God is doing. But God wants our lives to produce good fruit. The best we can give to Him. We can't do that when we are over-involved in activities—even good ones. So, God begins to prune our lives, guiding us into His best. Sometimes God's pruning is painful. But we can be sure that it is part of His process to make us fruitful.

92

MATERIALS NEEDED:

A grapevine with branches and leaves on it, or a tree or shrub branch with smaller branches and leaves on it; pruning shears.

INSTRUCTIONS:

Plan to arrive in the room before students. Place the vine or branch in a place where it won't be easily seen, but where it will be easily accessible.

Hold the vine or branch throughout the object lesson, referring to it often while pruning away leaves.

YOUR LIFE IS VALUABLE!

PRINCIPLE:

The most valuable gift a person can give to God is his or her life.

FOOD FOR THOUGHT:

Matthew 25:14-30; Romans 12:1,2; Ephesians 5:15-17; 1 Thessalonians 4:3-8; 1 Peter 4:7-11; 1 John 2:17

LESSON:

God has a will and purpose for each of us. He has given each of us special gifts and abilities with which we can serve Him. The most valuable gift any of us can give to God is to spend our lives for Him. Spending our lives for God gives us a value which cannot be taken away. But we have to make the choice. We can choose to invest our lives in godly things or we can choose to squander our lives on our own pursuits. If we follow our own desires, we can easily waste our lives.

MATERIALS NEEDED:

A few twenty-dollar bills (or larger depending on your budget and the economic status of your students), a small wastebasket, trash (empty food containers, paper, food, etc.).

INSTRUCTIONS:

Immediately after discussing the thoughts outlined in the lesson, pull out the bill and show it to your students. Say something like, "Here's a twenty-dollar bill. I'm considering giving this money to someone who can convince me that he or she will use it in a worthwhile manner. Tell me what you would use it for. Be honest; don't tell me you'll donate the money to a missionary fund if you're actually planning to use it to take a date to the movies."

After the students give their reponses, say, "You've given some very good ideas about how you would use the money if I were to give it to you. But this is *my* money to do with as *I* please. I could spend it on good things; perhaps I'll give it to an organization that helps feed the poor, or perhaps buy a gift for a friend. On the other hand, I could spend it on bad things; porn magazines, cigarettes or drugs. But instead, what I think I'll do is throw it away."

Give the students one more brief chance to suggest possible uses for the money. Then crumple the bill and throw it in the wastebasket. Your students will probably desperately try to persuade you to give them the money. Use the following comments as you repeat the process with another bill. "I know it frustrates you that I would waste something so valuable to you. Think how God must feel when we waste our lives, lives **He** created, lives for which He gave His only Son."

Ask the students at what point the bill would still be of value if you were to tear it into pieces. Let them guess. Then explain that there would have to be a little more than half of the bill left for it to have value. Explain, "With a bill we know when we have gone past the point of no return—the point when the money will no longer have value." Crumple another bill and throw it away. Say, "A human life is different from money, because we never know how much time we have on this earth. We may think we can ignore God and waste our lives on foolish pleasure while we're young and then when we're older, change our ways and live for Him. But none of us knows when the opportunity to turn our lives around will be ended by death. You or I could die tonight or tomorrow or next week, for all we know. We need to make the most of the time we have now so that we don't miss our chance to find the real value of life—serving God."

Put trash into the wastebasket over the crumpled bills and say, "You might think I've wasted this money by throwing it away, but it's worth every penny if even one person here decides to think seriously about what he is doing with his life. It's a terrible thing to waste one's life."